GROUPWORK IN DIVERSE CLASSROOMS:
A Casebook for Educators

Editors

Judith H. Shulman
WestEd

Rachel A. Lotan
Stanford University

Jennifer A. Whitcomb
University of Denver

Foreword

Linda Darling-Hammond

Published by Teachers College Press, 1234 Amsterdam Avenue, New York, NY 10027

Library of Congress Cataloging-in-Publication Data

Groupwork in diverse classrooms: a casebook for educators/Judith H. Shulman,
   Rachel A. Lotan, Jennifer A. Whitcomb [editors].
      p.   cm.
   Includes bibliographical references (p.).
   ISBN 0-8077-3701-1 (paper)
   1. Group work in education—United States—Case studies.
   2. Socially handicapped children—Education—United States—Case studies.
   3. Case method (Education) I. Shulman, Judith. II. Lotan, Rachel A.
   III. Whitcomb, Jennifer A.
   LB1032.G769 1998
   371.39′5—dc21   97-33507

Printed on acid-free paper
Manufactured in the United States of America

05 04 03 02 01 00 99 98   8 7 6 5 4 3 2 1

GROUPWORK IN DIVERSE CLASSROOMS:
A CASEBOOK FOR EDUCATORS

Editors

JUDITH H. SHULMAN
WestEd

RACHEL A. LOTAN
Stanford University

JENNIFER A. WHITCOMB
University of Denver

Foreword

LINDA DARLING-HAMMOND

Case Writers

CHRIS ALGER
DORIS ASH
MARIA DEL RIO
ANNE S. FROST
WERNER GARCIANO

DIANE KEPNER
SUZI MERCEIN
TOM MEYER
GRACE MORIZAWA
TOBY POLLOCK

KEN PORUSH
MARTY RUTHERFORD
SUSAN SCHULTZ
CAROLYN WADE
JILL WALKER

TEACHERS
COLLEGE
PRESS

Teachers College, Columbia University
New York and London

LIST OF CONTRIBUTORS

CHRIS ALGER, Claremont Middle School, Oakland Unified School District*

DORIS ASH, John Swett Elementary School, Oakland Unified School District*

MARIA DEL RIO, Alexander Rose Elementary School, Milpitas Unified School District*

ANNE S. FROST, Kennedy Middle School, Redwood City School District

WERNER GARCIANO, Capuchino High School, San Mateo Union High School District

DIANE KEPNER, Riverview Middle School, Mount Diablo Unified School District*

SUZI MERCEIN, Stanford Teacher Education Program, Stanford University*

TOM MEYER, Aragon High School, San Mateo Union High School District*

GRACE MORIZAWA, Emerson Elementary School, Oakland Unified School District*

TOBY POLLOCK, Kennedy Middle School, Redwood City Unified School District

KEN PORUSH, Steinbeck Middle School, San Jose Unified School District*

MARTY RUTHERFORD, John Swett Elementary School, Oakland Unified School District*

SUSAN SCHULTZ, Menlo-Atherton High School, Sequoia Union High School District*

CAROLYN WADE, Carlmont High School, Sequoia High School District*

JILL WALKER, John Swett Elementary School, Oakland Unified School District

---

*These case writers have moved on to new school/work assignments since this casebook project was begun.

TABLE OF CONTENTS

FOREWORD

Even under the simplest of circumstances, teaching is one of the most complex jobs imaginable. Teachers must juggle a wide array of curriculum goals with the social demands of managing a group of 25 or 30 students while attending to their individual needs. They must garner cooperation from young "conscripted" workers, as Dan Lortie noted in *Schoolteacher* thirty years ago. And they must do so in a fashion that not only produces order but results in profitable intellectual work.

These demands have typically led to curriculum and instructional strategies that simplify teaching, but, unfortunately, reduce cognitive demands and student initiation of learning activities at the same time. Teacher-delivered lectures and individual seatwork defined by text questions and worksheets predominate in American classrooms. These tactics are favored in large part because they make teaching more manageable, and they increase the sense of predictability in a highly uncertain endeavor.

Yet this traditional pedagogy, we have learned, is inadequate for many educational goals that are increasing in importance. As our society and economy become ever more complex, young people must learn how to access and use resources, to frame and solve problems, to organize work with others, to pursue hypotheses, and to redirect their efforts as needed. In tomorrow's labor market, most will be headed for "knowledge-based" jobs in which they must plan and evaluate their own work, organize team efforts, and continually learn changing skills and technologies, rather than facing the routine tasks planned by others that were the norm in the factories, farms, and mills of the past.

Young people cannot learn these things if their school-work never asks them to engage in such tasks. And learning to work in a self-organized fashion with other human beings who operate differently is a long-term undertaking that takes considerable practice over many months and years. Groupwork is essential to these goals and to others: for example, extending learning opportunities for many students through peer teaching, which is a potential solution to the limits on teacher time and attention. Yet managing groups of students engaged in complex intellectual tasks is difficult and complicated work for which most teachers have not been prepared.

Hence, the value of this enormously useful casebook, which describes the dilemmas and the possibilities of groupwork from the teacher's view, using classroom conundrums as the basis for deliberation. This interesting and provocative volume could not have arrived at a better time. As teachers across the country are intensely engaged in developing new pedagogies that seek to teach all students for deeper levels of understanding, they are confronting the real world obstacles that theoreticians and policymakers sometimes gloss over when they urge classroom reforms.

Although organizing students to engage in more challenging intellectual inquiry may be imperative to achieve the new educational standards policymakers propose, it is much more uncertain work than marching through the text. What do teachers do, for example, when groups seem unable to get organized? When some students dominate and others withdraw? When students have trouble getting along? When the lofty goals of complex projects seem imperfectly attained? How does a teacher know exactly what students are learning as they pursue their own research, debate ideas, and develop their own ways of presenting their knowledge?

Such questions require teachers to develop what I call "two-way pedagogies" — tactics for looking and listening to students that help them learn what students are thinking and feeling as well as what they are learning. In addition, teachers need to be able to examine the results of their efforts as do the authors in this book, to evaluate strategies and imagine alternatives. These tactics are even more necessary in very diverse class-rooms where students may require different kinds of scaffolding to engage in group learning that demands critical thinking, initiative, and ongoing problem solving. Traditionally, schools have been organized to offer such opportunities only to the 10% or 20% of students presumed to be headed for "thinking work" — those who are tracked into gifted and talented, honors, or advanced courses, who learn easily in the ways schools normally teach and who can teach themselves even when pedagogy fails.

Now that society demands such abilities of most citizens instead of only a few, schools must learn how to teach challenging content and complex skills to students who come with a wide range of experiences, skills, and learning styles — including students who rely less on the traditional verbal pathways that school has empha-sized, those who have serious learning difficulties, and those whose language background or home experiences differ from typical school norms.

Groupwork in Diverse Classrooms takes on all of these concerns and others. The first chapter offers a superb overview of research and problems of practice associ-ated with groupwork, especially when it is aimed at teaching for understanding. Then, using diverse teach-ing and learning situations as sites for discussion, this volume offers cases developed by teachers in elemen-tary and secondary classrooms in a variety of settings, pursuing a range of teaching goals.

Teachers and teacher educators will find *Groupwork in Diverse Classrooms* helpful for considering issues of theory in practice, as a means for teachers to consider and debate teaching decisions with one another, to learn from the wisdom of practice, and to link research to real classroom issues. The *Facilitator's Guide* is an added gift, offering strategies for using the cases to raise funda-mental issues and to consider alternative perspectives. Together, they provide grist for the deliberations that are at the heart of teaching: given what we know and what we can learn, what does one do in this situation with these students and this set of concerns? Using research and inquiry to help teachers learn about practice in practice is at the crux of a profession, and what will ultimately make the difference for students.

Linda Darling-Hammond

This volume is the fifth in a series of teacher-written casebooks developed at the Far West Laboratory (now known as WestEd[*]). These casebooks are part of a nation-wide effort to capture and use practitioner knowledge to better prepare teachers for the reality of today's class-rooms.

Unlike business, law, and medicine, education has made little formal use of cases as professional training tools. But interest in case-based teaching is now growing in both teacher preparation and in-service training pro-grams. The 1980s reform movement is largely respon-sible for this growing interest. During the effort to improve schools, it has become increasingly clear that teachers are unprepared for the huge array of challenges presented by a student population and workplace vastly different from that of even a decade ago. Novices often find the gritty, real-life classroom to be light years from the ideal they had imagined as students. Spotlighting this gap between theory and practice, the 1986 Carnegie report *A Nation Prepared: Teachers for the Twenty-First Century* recommended that teacher training institutions use "cases illustrating a great variety of teaching prob-lems" as "a major focus of instruction" (p. 76).

What do we mean by "case"? Cases are candid, dra-matic, highly readable accounts of teaching events or series of events. They show a problem-based snapshot of an on-the-job dilemma. Read alone, cases offer the vicarious experience of walking in another's shoes. In group discussion, they are especially powerful, allowing differing points of view to be aired and examined. For that reason, cases are consciously designed to provoke discussion that is engaging, demanding, and intellectu-

---

[*] WestEd was created in 1996 as a merger of two regional educa-tional laboratories, Far West Laboratory for Educational Research and Development (FWL) and Southwest Regional Laboratory (SWRL).

ally exciting. Some cases are written by researchers, but those we have pioneered over the past ten years at WestEd are written by teachers themselves.

Because they tell vivid, moving stories, cases give life to abstract principles and propositions, and are likely to be remembered. Teacher educators, administrators, men-tors, and staff developers use cases to trigger discussion about why a given strategy works or does not work. Beginners learn to create lessons that promote learning and environments that promote safety and trust. They learn to frame problems from multiple perspectives, interpret complex situations, and identify decision points and possible consequences—that is, they learn to think like teachers. Veterans discuss teaching situations that mirror their own, in the process reflecting on their values, attitudes, and assumptions and wrestling with the disequilibrium this creates. As a result, they often change or broaden their beliefs about teaching and learning, and thus adopt very different ways of working with students.

WestEd's Approach

The WestEd case writing process makes practitioners themselves the subjects, producers, and consumers of action research. We emphasize this because teachers generally have few mechanisms to record and preserve their accumulated knowledge. When a teacher retires or leaves the profession, her understanding, methods, and materials—which should form a legacy to the profession, the community, and the school—are generally lost. Today, however, there is an expanding literature on the practitioner experience. The casebooks contribute to it by combining the growing body of research about teaching with specific accounts of classroom dilemmas written by teachers themselves.

Cases are not simply narrative descriptions of events. To call something a case is to make a theoretical claim—that it is a case *of* something, or an instance of a larger class. This is not to say that all cases illustrate, exemplify, or teach a theoretical principle. To be valuable as a case, however, the narrative should be representative of a class or type of dilemma, problem or quandary that arises with some frequency in teaching situations. Most rich cases are cases "of" many things. Cases may also be exemplars of principles, describing by their detail a general pattern of practice.

The narratives in our casebooks are selected because they meet the criterion representing a larger class of experiences. In our first volume, *The Mentor Teacher Casebook*, 22 mentor teachers from the Los Angeles Unified School District (LAUSD) describe the rewards and frustrations of providing on-the-job assistance to beginning teachers. An outgrowth of our study of the California Mentor Teacher Program's first year, its vignettes describe how the mentor–colleague relationship develops and illustrate the complexity of the new mentor role. In the second casebook, *The Intern Teacher Casebook*, first-year teachers—again in LAUSD—describe in frank and moving detail the reality shock they experienced during their first few months instructing teenagers in inner-city schools. The stories frequently reveal their initial inability to understand youngsters with backgrounds radically different from their own. They also portray the enormous challenge of simultaneously encountering two new cultures: teaching and poverty.

Our third volume, *Diversity in the Classroom: A Casebook for Teachers and Teacher Educators*, continues the focus on diversity, but from the perspective of veteran teachers who describe some of the most problematic experiences of their careers. Some look back to their novice days, describe how they handled a situation, and reflect on what they might do differently now. Others relate current concerns and leave us with unresolved problems.

About This Casebook

The 16 cases in the pages that follow are again set in diverse, predominantly low-income schools. All but two are written by veteran teachers who describe the challenges and dilemmas of using groupwork in their classrooms. All of these teachers are committed to the benefits of groupwork. Some veterans have been exploring multiple approaches for several years, while others are in the midst of transforming their teaching. Whatever the degree of experience, all would agree that using groupwork effectively is a complex and time-consuming skill. It demands preparation activities that build classroom community and collaborative working relationships among students, group tasks that require a contribution from each group member, and curriculum that shows coherence among the group tasks. Even with the best of intentions and planning, things can go awry in the messy world of practice—students are absent, behave differently than anticipated, or may not like to work in groups.

To stimulate analysis and reflection, these cases focus on the surprises—the unanticipated events that happen every day in classrooms. The particular problems represented in the narratives were carefully chosen by the teachers because they hoped that others could learn from their experiences. As you will note when you read and discuss the cases, they often embed many of the same dilemmas that involve:

- examining why and how to use groupwork effectively;

- designing group tasks that both complement one another and demand contributions from all group members;

- analyzing the appropriate role of a teacher during group activities;

- exploring constructive teacher interventions during group process;

- crafting groups that support learning for all students;

- supporting students to help them cooperate and collaborate with one another;

- dealing with uncooperative individuals and groups of students;

- providing effective status interventions;

- developing appropriate assessments for group activities; and

- exploring how to communicate with parents who may be critical of group projects.

We have tried to sequence the cases to highlight many of these dilemmas. But since cases are usually "of" many things, they often don't fit neatly in any one chapter or section (see Table 1, Overview of Issues Across Cases).

For those interested in pursuing additional reading, we offer an Annotated Bibliography on Groupwork at the end of this volume. If you are interested in adapting our case development methodology to create your own set of cases, please look at the guidelines we used with contributors to this casebook in the Appendix.

TIPS FOR USING THESE CASES

Recent reforms in education promote the use of groupwork in heterogeneous classrooms. Yet we and the contributors to this book appreciate the difficulty and complexity of utilizing groupwork effectively. We hope that these cases will prompt you and your colleagues to be more reflective and analytical about how to design and implement appropriate group tasks. We also hope you will analyze how to create a community of learners characterized by norms of cooperation and collaboration, a coherent curriculum that leads to deep understanding of the subject matter, and tasks that engage group members in a meaningful pursuit of learning.

As stated above, cases are powerful discussion catalysts. Good discussion can help people dig into a case. As you read these cases, you may want to ask yourself questions such as: How did the teacher frame the problems he encountered? In what other ways could the problem have been framed? What did this teacher actually do and why? With what result? What alternative strategies might have been tried? At what risk? With what consequences? What were students thinking and feeling? How did they try to communicate this to the teacher? How does this teacher's story parallel experiences of your own? How might this case (or case discussion) lead you to think of different ways of dealing with these dilemmas? What principles of teaching and learning can be generated from your analysis?

The *Facilitator's Guide* has been prepared to accompany this casebook. It was developed as a result of a pilot test of all the cases with a variety of educational groups. It includes an analysis of issues embedded in each case and sample questions to raise during a discussion. Deliberations stimulated from such questions can help people to:

1. spot issues and frame problems in ambiguous situations;

2. interpret situations from multiple perspectives;

3. identify crucial decision points and possibilities for action;

4. recognize potential risks and benefits inherent in any course of action; and

5. identify and test teaching principles in real classroom situations.

AN INVITATION TO JOIN US

Unlike cases in previous casebooks, those in this edition are not accompanied by commentaries. During our field test of each case, we gained new insights by engaging in stimulating discussions with a variety of educators. Consequently, we decided to try an experiment to broaden the discourse by inviting you to join us. Instead of our soliciting commentaries from other educators, we invite you to write your own reactions and interpretations to each case and enter them on the World Wide Web site created at WestEd, *http:// www.WestEd.org/icd* or send an email message to *icd@WestEd.org*. We hope to encourage analysis of cases *and* of case discussions. Utilizing the Internet, we can exceed the boundaries of any individual analysis and create a community of learners for all who use the cases.

Judith H. Shulman

Table 1

Overview of Issues Across Cases

Case No.	Purposes for groupwork	Design of groupwork tasks	Assessment	Role of the teacher	When and how to intervene	Crafting groups	Use of student roles	Supporting cooperation and collaboration	Uncooperative students/group/class	Status problems	Status interventions	Communication with parents and other teachers	Groupwork in professional development	English learners
Case 1	X			X	X			X		X				
Case 2	X	X	X											
Case 3	X	X				X	X		X					
Case 4	X	X	X	X	X		X	X	X					
Case 5	X	X	X										X	
Case 6	X	X		X	X	X		X		X	X			X
Case 7		X	X	X	X	X	X			X				
Case 8		X		X	X			X		X			X	
Case 9	X	X		X	X	X	X	X						
Case 10	X	X		X	X			X	X					
Case 11	X	X	X	X				X	X	X	X			
Case 12		X	X	X		X		X		X	X			
Case 13	X	X		X			X	X		X	X			X
Case 14	X	X	X									X		
Case 15		X				X		X		X		X	X	
Case 16	X	X	X	X	X		X	X	X	X	X			X

Table 1. Overview of Issues Across Cases

ACKNOWLEDGMENTS

We would first like to thank the case writers for taking time out of their busy schedules to write such interesting and candid accounts. These teachers had the courage to both question their beliefs and document their perceptions through multiple drafts of their cases. Thanks also for invaluable input from Nikola Filby and Carne Barnett, WestEd colleagues; advisory board members Elizabeth Cohen, Joe Campione, Deborah Edginton, Amalia Mesa-Bains, Pam Tyson, Bettye Haysbert, Susana Mata, and Susan McBride, who provided wisdom and asked difficult questions; and Don Barfield, who supported this project from its inception.

Several other people made valuable contributions: Rosemary De La Torre, who kept us organized throughout the project and revised multiple drafts; Kim O'Neill, who developed the annotated bibliography; Joy Zimmerman and Sally Ianiro, our WestEd editors and most insightful critics; and Sarah J. Biondello and Carol Collins, Teachers College Press editors, whose insights helped to refine the manuscript. Special thanks go to our spouses, Lee, Zohar, and John, who supported us through every step of the way

Judith H. Shulman
Rachel A. Lotan
Jennifer A. Whitcomb

INTRODUCTION

Groupwork in Diverse Classrooms

Rachel A. Lotan
Jennifer A. Whitcomb

Groupwork is a well-documented and highly recommended strategy for enhancing academic, cognitive, social, and attitudinal outcomes for students. Researchers (Cohen & Lotan, 1997; Sharan, 1994; Slavin, 1990) have shown that students who experience groupwork make greater learning gains in basic academic skills as well as higher-order thinking when compared to students in traditional whole-class instruction. Students who learn in groups also demonstrate enhanced social skills and interracial, interethnic acceptance. Thus groupwork is considered a sound instructional approach for academically, ethnically, and linguistically heterogeneous classrooms. In these diverse settings, students can serve as resources to one another as they complete intellectually challenging learning tasks.

When students engage in meaningful groupwork tasks, they pose interesting and original questions, make hypotheses or tentative interpretations, deliberate over ideas and how to accomplish a task, and learn to resolve conflicts that are both intellectual and social in nature. In short, in the company of others, individuals construct deeper understandings of concepts. Psychologists agree that social interactions shape enduring learning; thus groupwork is one important setting for such interactions to unfold.

In this chapter we provide a brief overview of the major issues related to groupwork as an instructional strategy and relate them to particular cases in this volume. The issues we address are:

1. organization of the classroom for groupwork and the necessary redefinition of the traditional roles of teacher and students;

2. features of a sound group task;

3. unequal status and unequal participation of members of a group;

4. assessment in groupwork; and

5. organizational support and professional development for teachers using groupwork.

ORGANIZATION OF THE CLASSROOM FOR GROUPWORK

During groupwork, the organization of the classroom is vastly different from the structure of the classroom in whole-class or individualized instruction. When six to eight groups are in simultaneous operation, it becomes impractical, if not physically impossible, for a teacher to supervise all the groups personally. She cannot single-handedly see to it that groups run smoothly and that students understand what needs to be done and how best to complete the task. The teacher cannot (nor should she) take for granted that all students benefit equally from group processes and/or contribute substantially to the group product.

This structural change in classroom organization necessitates changes in its management and redefinitions of the traditional roles of teacher and student. When students work in groups, the teacher is no longer the focal point in the classroom, the sole provider of information and knowledge, constantly regulating and closely directing students' behavior and learning. Instead, students become responsible for their own learning and that of their group mates. Cohen (1994a, b) calls this process "delegating authority," meaning that the teacher delegates to the groups and to the individuals in these groups, the authority and the responsibility both for managing the group and for ensuring group members' engagement in learning as well as completion of the task (1994a, p. 104).

Redefining their traditional role doesn't come easily for many teachers. Some struggle with no longer being "the center of this steadily revolving wheel" (see Case 16). Others worry that without their constant supervision, the classroom might deteriorate into chaos, i.e., students will not understand what needs to be done, they will make too many mistakes, and/or they won't complete their assignments. When teachers delegate authority, they poignantly ask themselves how far such delegation of authority can and should go. For instance, in Case 1 the author asks herself when and how to intervene when students "as teachers" present incorrect information. In Cases 4 and 10, the teachers are taken aback by some students' reluctance and resistance to accept the authority delegated to them. Having decided that they will not rescue the groups, these authors wrestle with the pain of watching their students "fail." The teacher–author of Case 9 refuses to become the referee when two students are unable to resolve a conflict in their group. He orders them to "come up with a plan of action that [will] allow them to complete the rest of the lab the next day." In a similar situation, the author of Case 8 resolves the conflict by separating the adversaries.

When the teacher successfully delegates authority, students talk and work together to find out what they are expected to do and how they should go about solving the challenging problems assigned to them. When students engage in groupwork on intellectually challenging tasks, the more they talk and work together, the more they learn (Cohen, Lotan, & Holthuis, 1995; Cohen, Lotan, & Leechor, 1989).

Just as redefining the role of the teacher creates its own challenges, so does redefining the role of the student. Working in groups comes neither naturally nor easily for many of us. Asking for help or assisting classmates who ask for help used to be called "cheating," and was (and in many settings still is) heavily penalized. Individual effort and accomplishment are still highly rewarded both in schools and in society. For productive groupwork, students need to learn new and different social skills: how to ask for help and how to assist others who do, how to explain patiently, how to be productive and responsible group members, and how to respect and value other people's contributions. Educators found that for students to work in groups success-

fully, skills for cooperation, collaboration, and conflict resolution need to be taught explicitly and practiced consistently before they become internalized, routine group behaviors. Several cases (e.g., 4 and 6) allude to measures the teachers took to prepare their classes to handle social and intellectual exchanges in the group.

By assigning each student a specific procedural role (e.g., facilitator, materials manager, timer, reporter, recorder, safety officer, and encourager) the teacher is able to better delegate authority (Ehrlich & Zack, 1997). Every member of the group plays a different role, and roles rotate. For example, the facilitator sees to it that everyone understands what to do, gets help when necessary, and participates in group interactions. The recorder keeps notes of the group's discussions and checks to see if individual reports have been completed. The materials manager makes sure that the group has all the equipment necessary and that the tables are cleared at the end of the lesson. Some teachers assign roles randomly (Case 7), some match roles to students' perceived personalities (Case 8), and others rotate them so students learn to perform all roles (Case 16). Unlike these procedural roles, other kinds of roles teachers assign relate to the substance of the group activity. For example, for a task of preparing a multimedia presentation on a certain topic, the roles assigned to the students might be director, narrator, coordinator, document analyst, and community liaison. In this example the roles serve to divide the labor by having each student accomplish a substantive portion of the task at hand.

When well implemented, roles can assure that groups run smoothly and that individuals know what needs to be done. However, like learning how to cooperate, playing the roles well will not happen naturally for students. To learn the behaviors that accompany each role, students need to recognize, discuss, and practice the specific responsibilities of each role. Many teachers find the use of roles helpful as they take care of the many necessary yet mundane minutiae of instruction, not only freeing the teacher of the burden of micromanaging groups but also allowing him to turn his attention to the real business of teaching: probing for understanding, delving into the content, and stimulating and extending students' thinking. Many of the cases in this volume illustrate how delegation of authority is a constant negotiation between teacher and student or between student and student, and the teacher's conflicting and at times contradictory views of his own pedagogical identity.

LEARNING TASKS FOR PRODUCTIVE GROUPWORK

An often underestimated predictor of a successful groupwork lesson is a sound group task. Sound problem solving group tasks have four distinct features:

1. uncertainty;

2. multiple abilities;

3. group interdependence and individual accountability; and

4. an organizing "big idea."

Uncertainty

Researchers distinguish between problem solving, open-ended "ill-structured" tasks (e.g., designing an experiment, explicating a text, solving mathematical problems in real-life contexts, reconciling different points of view) and routine tasks (e.g., decoding, recalling factual information, completing worksheets). Others distinguish between purely linguistic tasks or tasks that require only traditional academic skills (reading, writing, computing) and tasks that require many different intellectual abilities for their successful completion. (For a review see Cohen, 1994c; Lotan, 1997.)

Routine tasks have clearly defined procedures or steps that need to be followed and usually a right or wrong answer. Students can carry out such tasks by conscientiously heeding instructions, completing sentences, applying familiar algorithms and formulas, and finding and memorizing information. While groupwork might not be essential for completing such tasks, it can benefit many students. Some researchers (e.g., Webb, 1982) have documented the academic benefits for those students who provide help to their peers by explaining, modeling, and practicing these skills while accomplishing such routine paper-and-pencil tasks. In contrast, when students engage in problem solving, open-ended, and hands-on activities, they grapple with many uncertainties: they explore different alternatives and often come up with legitimately different solutions. In a recent synthesis of research, Qin, Johnson, and Johnson (1995) found that cooperation in hands-on activities enhances problem solving when compared to linguistic tasks, i.e., tasks that rely on verbal interaction exclusively.

Sound group tasks are as close as possible to real-life situations, genuine problems, or authentic dilemmas. Like real life, such group tasks are uncertain both in their outcome and in the ways one can go about identifying strategies and finding solutions; open-ended questions and problem solving activities ask for students' experiences, opinions, and interpretations. Beyond the who, where, and what, students reflect on why and how things happened as they did and whether they could have happened differently. In such activities, students analyze and evaluate, discuss cause and effect, explore controversial issues, and draw conclusions. Lotan (1997) argues that "by assigning tasks that are open-ended in their process and in their outcome, teachers effectively delegate *intellectual authority* to the students" (p.110, emphasis in original). However, this delegation of intellectual authority is often difficult for teachers who might be confronted by their students' unexpected and sometimes uncomfortable answers or solutions. Many teachers try to maintain control of their students' intellectual enterprise through tight supervision of the learning task by overspecifying instructions or by preteaching the assignment to remove much of the uncertainty.

Many teachers have found that, like them, students handle a task's uncertainty with varying degrees of comfort and success. Although some groups proceed with no major flare-ups, particularly if they've been carefully prepared for groupwork, many find more than one legitimate outcome and more than one possible solution frustrating, if not infuriating. In Case 2, the teacher had hoped that through "observation and interaction" and by "working together to map the rat's movements, [her second grade] students would look more closely . . . and begin to speculate together." However, after the group had been unable to complete this activity, the teacher assigned a task that more "closely mirrored the kind of work [students] routinely did in their classrooms: looking up answers to questions in a book." The teacher reflects on the outcome of her case: "Students called the more traditional reading and question–answer activities 'real learning.' Hands-on groupwork often required interaction that sent the room through increasingly uncomfortable noise levels amplified by the wooden ceiling and walls, threatening classroom order. Students didn't associate groupwork—even when it was successful—with real learning. I wonder if students feel less secure generating their own questions and finding answers from multiple resources than when they are working with questions and 'real' answers from a textbook. What can I do to expand their concept of 'real learning'?"

Similarly, the teacher–author of Case 4 expresses her surprise and disappointment "at the extent to which students [in a high school chemistry class] depend on [her] to confirm their ideas and to acknowledge that they are somehow correct or right. They are locked into learning the right answer, are often unable to adequately debate an opinion in contrast to their own, and seem totally unaware of the importance of the problem solving process. Most students define learning as knowing a collection of right answers." This teacher decides to challenge her students' "narrow definition of learning" by giving them opportunities to "learn as much from the process of identifying problems, hypoth-esizing solutions, analyzing the consequences of probable answers, and deciding upon a plan of action as they learn from the final solution."

Often teachers need to convince parents that open-ended group tasks are legitimate learning assignments. When the intern teacher in Case 14 creates a nonconventional task for her high school students, a parent sends the following message: "Now, I remember hokey stuff like that from my own elementary school days several hundred years ago: a quiz show featuring food, clothing, and shelter of Peru. But this is high school. Are the kids incapable of learning without entertainment? . . . Do I misunderstand? Were the kids staging an elaborate hoax on an impressionable parent to make him believe that there's so much time in the school year that you have the liberty to engage in this crap . . . [and] fluff?"

As the sine qua non of group tasks, uncertainty of the outcome and the multiplicity of ways to complete a task or resolve a problem challenge students' as well as teachers' (and often parents') conceptions of learning. This challenge can produce great anxiety and even resistance.

Multiple abilities

Rich group tasks also require many different skills and multiple intellectual abilities for their successful completion. Such tasks allow students to contribute their various talents, multiple intelligences (see Gardner, 1983), or diverse repertoire of problem solving strategies; they also provide students with opportunities to develop these strengths further and to acquire new ones. When tasks are multidimensional, more students have more opportunities to show intellectual competence. By making tasks multidimensional rather than unidimensional along the basic academic skills of reading and writing, educators are redefining not only the learning task but also the traditional social system of the classroom by which students are divided roughly into two categories: "smart" and "dumb." Multidimensional multiple-ability tasks are a precondition for providing more opportunities for more students to show "smarts" and be perceived as smart by the teacher and by their peers.

Group tasks that include multiple abilities can serve an additional purpose: they attract more students to the task and entice them to participate, thus opening additional avenues for students to gain access to the learning task. Students who are still learning to read might be drawn to a multiple-ability task by examining and analyzing a photograph or a video clip. Some students might be lured to the task and respond more readily when listening to an audiotape of a song, speech, or story. Students who are in the process of learning the language of instruction might understand a task better as they work with real objects, manipulatives, or three-dimensional models in addition to attending to verbal information. Students who still have difficulty reading might access information—related to the activity from a graph, matrix, cartoon, or diagram—that has traditionally been conveyed exclusively through text. For instance, when the task was to design a sturdy structure, the central student in Case 13, Miguel (who could neither speak English nor read the instructions to the task), discovered that the base required reinforcement after studying the diagram included on the activity card.

Many students who are turned off by traditional learning activities show improvement in reading and writing when given the opportunity to participate through these alternate routes. Through participation in multiple-ability learning activities, these students are practicing traditional academic skills in a meaningful context, for "real" reasons: to understand, to communicate, and to contribute. The intern teacher in Case 14 designed a multiple-ability unit that addresses "connections between Renaissance art and the major intellectual themes of the period." After completing the unit, students wrote individual essays. The teacher comments: "I received quality test essays, even from those who usually have problems on traditional assessments. I am satisfied with the value of kinesthetic assignments and will incorporate them in the future. These outcomes seem to corroborate arguments that multiple-ability tasks reach more students than those that fit the verbal learning style category."

Multiple-ability tasks, then, extend and broaden teachers' and students' conceptions of intelligence, of "smarts." As more students contribute to the group's efforts, feel efficacious, and are seen and recognized as intellectually competent by their peers and by the teacher, the social system of the classroom is dramatically altered.

Interdependence and individual accountability

By definition, group tasks need to create and support interdependence among members of a group. Positive interdependence is the essence of collaboration (Johnson & Johnson, 1994). If a single student were able to complete a task by herself, there would be scant incentive for groupwork, since groupwork usually requires extra effort and is often less time efficient than individual work. Interdependence is enhanced when students are accountable for a group product to which all members have contributed. When tasks are sufficiently rich, i.e., open-ended and consisting of multiple abilities, when there is a limit on the amount of time the teacher and the class can devote to the activity, and when the teacher can create a sense of urgency regarding groupwork, then students will have to rely on one another to understand and complete the task. The teacher–author of Case 9 describes how a group "blew up" not only because two students didn't get along socially, but also because "there wasn't enough in this lab to keep five people engaged, a situation that had caused a lot of the initial frustration."

Reaching consensus can be seen as a product of the group's collaboration. However, groups are often unable to reach an agreement or come to a consensus all members can embrace. In Case 7, the teacher laments the fact that because members of a group failed to reach consensus, they never achieved the degree of interdependence he was hoping for. Hence, from the teacher's perspective, although the students' individual essays were strong, the group's presentation was weak in content and dominated by two of the students, and "the other two never really found their way into the project." Clearly there was no real interdependence in this group.

Though interdependence is built into rich group tasks, teachers also worry about holding each student personally accountable for contributing to the group's success and mastering the concepts embedded in the activity (e.g., Cases 2, 4, and 16). Written reports completed individually after a group activity are often a means for ensuring such accountability.

Big idea

As mentioned, groupwork is particularly beneficial when conceptual learning, problem solving, and deep understanding of content and subject matter are the goals of instruction. To learn central concepts or big ideas of a discipline, students need to have the opportunity to interact and to discuss and clarify their thoughts about such content. That is why well-designed group activities address a big idea, speak to an essential question, or invoke a central disciplinary concept with which students will grapple. For example, Cases 1 and 12 are both built around groupwork lessons in which students address interdependence in the natural world, a central concept in the biological sciences. They do so through the particular problem of using pesticides and their effects on endangered species on the island of Borneo.

Well-crafted group activities are excellent opportunities for students to examine central concepts and big questions from different perspectives and to propose different solutions. For example, the teacher–author of Case 5 designed a unit in which students explore the concept of density in various settings. However, this example of "less is more" created a further dilemma. Whereas previously the teacher had devoted but a single period to the difficult concept of density, when using groupwork she devoted over four days to exploring the same concept, albeit in different contexts and with different problems. This dilemma of breadth (i.e., content coverage) versus depth (i.e., conceptual learning) is also addressed by the teacher–author of Case 14.

Developing sound group tasks requires much time and effort and many resources. Because creating such a curriculum is an uncertain endeavor, teachers benefit from collaboration with fellow teachers and subject matter experts. Furthermore, the development of sound tasks is often a powerful setting for teachers' professional development: by creating appropriate tasks, they deepen their understanding of the social and intellectual processes involved in groupwork.

EQUAL ACCESS AND PARTICIPATION

Many teachers dread the uncomfortable yet painfully familiar situation in groupwork when one student dominates the interaction and takes over the group. Alternatively, another student withdraws from the group and sits quietly and unobtrusively at best, or becomes disruptive and sabotages other people's work at worst. Many teachers notice that those students who are seen as smart and popular (i.e., high-status students) participate more in groupwork than those who are perceived as weak in the subject matter and who have few or no friends (i.e., low-status students). Cohen (1982) has called this relationship between status and rate of participation in small group settings a status problem. Unless educators address this problem and break this well-documented connection between status and participation that leads to learning (Cohen & Lotan, 1995; Cohen, Lotan, & Catanzarite, 1990), the learning gap increases.

Explicitly or implicitly, a number of teacher–authors in this casebook touch upon dilemmas concerning unequal opportunities for students to learn, to participate, or to have access to instructional materials. The teacher–authors vividly recall their worries, anxieties, or feelings of sheer helplessness in their interactions with students who have low academic skills (Cases 10, 11, and 13); who are divergent thinkers and behave differently from everyone else in the class (Case 12); who are newcomers and don't speak the language (Cases 7 and 16); or who have the uncanny ability to "push a teacher's buttons" (Case 8). More than anything, these teachers would like to be able to address these problems of status successfully, to provide all students with equal opportunities for learning and academic success.

Some of our teacher–authors recount their experiences with Complex Instruction, a model of groupwork in which status problems are addressed directly and explicitly. In Cases 11, 13, and 16, the authors describe specific interventions designed to equalize status and participation. For example, in Case 13, the teacher explains how and why she uses multiple-ability tasks and how she orients her students: "Whenever we do groupwork, I choose activities complex enough to require many different abilities. To complete a task, a group needs students skilled in reading and writing, but also those with other abilities, such as balancing, building, drawing, estimating, hypothesizing, and measuring." Having chosen such a task, she clarifies her intention to her students: "Every member of the group can use at least one of his abilities and can contribute to completion of the task." In Complex Instruction, such clarification and explanation is called a "multiple-ability orientation." Once students recognize the range of "smarts" necessary to complete a group activity, teachers can use an additional strategy called "assigning competence." The author describes this strategy as follows: "I use specific strategies to encourage students to use their many abilities and to recognize them for doing so. For example, I observe them as they work in groups and give very specific and public feedback. I also show how what they've done is critical to the task at hand and how they contributed to their group."

In Case 16, the teacher describes the outcome of a successful status intervention: "Roberto was one who had made much improvement. He spoke up more frequently, and as I pointed out the value of his contributions, others in the class began to take his opinions more seriously. He was by no means a great student, but he was no longer failing."

Once teachers understand the importance of status interventions, they are committed to enacting them. The teacher–author of Case 11 writes, "Knowing that the low expectations of his peers would inhibit Dennis's ability to participate fully in the small group projects, I planned to alter their expectations by assigning competence to Dennis, whenever possible taking special care to point out his intellectual abilities. This is the opposite of the 'pull yourself up by your bootstraps' approach teachers often use with students in groupwork." Despite such hearty commitments though, the same teacher reveals the painful insight that the promise of these intervention strategies is not realized with every student.

ASSESSMENT IN GROUPWORK

Although assessment "raises tough questions with many unresolved answers" (see Case 5), it has garnered much attention in recent years. In this case, the teacher addresses the lack of a match between the mode of instruction she was using—groupwork, which relies on collaboration and open-ended tasks around the concept of density—and the quiz she used to assess students' understanding (a multiple-choice, individual test in which students were asked to use formulas to calculate density). This lack of a tight connection between instruction and assessment led to grave disappointment: although both teacher and students spent much time and effort on the unit, students did no better on the quiz than had students in previous years, when the teacher had devoted only one period to the concept of density. After much soul-searching, the teacher and her students realized that the tools for assessment needed to be more closely aligned with the purposes and the content of groupwork. On a second quiz, when students themselves participated in its design, when criteria for evaluation were clear from the beginning, students' achievements improved.

In addition to the problem of closely connecting what one teaches to what one tests for, many more questions arise around assessment of groupwork and many of the cases touch on important dilemmas: When assessing the quality of a group product, does a teacher assign a group grade or an individual grade? How can a teacher be sure of the relative contribution of each member of a group? What about the "social loafers," the "free riders," and the "suckers," of whom others take advantage? How will the teacher assess competence of individuals in their thinking skills and in subject matter knowledge after group collaboration? What are the important social skills related to groupwork, and how will the teacher measure students' ability to communicate, make decisions, negotiate, resolve conflicts—in short, collaborate productively and function effectively as members of a team?

In a recent article, Webb (1995) reviews the dilemmas surrounding two different, sometimes competing goals of groupwork: group productivity versus individual learning.

> When the goal of groupwork is group productivity, evaluation focuses on the output of the group. Either the quantity of output, or the quality of the product, or both, may be evaluated (for example, the quantity of ideas for solving a problem, the quality of a solution to a problem). When the goal of groupwork is learning on the part of individual members, in contrast, evaluation focuses on learning outcomes, not the quality of the group's performance on the group task…. Because the processes and outcomes of group collaboration may differ depending on whether the goal is individual learning or group productivity, it is important that the purpose of the assessment, the goal of group work and the group processes supposed to contribute to those goals be specified clearly. (p. 241)

To motivate their students, some teachers grade them on individual participation in groupwork. However, a note of caution is in order: as explained earlier, students may be hampered in their participation not because they lack motivation or willingness to participate. Often they are shut out from the group and ignored by their peers because of the existence of a status problem. In such cases it would be quite unfair to blame these students, admonish them for not putting out enough effort, or punish them by lowering their grades.

ORGANIZATIONAL SUPPORT AND PROFESSIONAL DEVELOPMENT

Few of the teacher–authors explicitly address how the context of their school influences their use of groupwork. Yet educational research and policy communities, as well as teachers and administrators, recognize that organizational support is crucial for successful implementation of sophisticated pedagogy, such as groupwork. At the school site, the principal plays a critical role in purchasing, organizing, and coordinating the use of materials that are essential for group tasks: manipulatives for mathematics and science classrooms, art supplies, and library and technology resources. Many teachers find that longer class periods are more conducive to groupwork than the typical 50-minute period. Thus the principal needs to consider the length of class periods when designing the school schedule. A further consideration in the design of the master schedule is structuring regular time for colleagues to meet for curriculum planning and reflection. Finally, the principal, as instructional leader, communicates to the teachers and to the outside community (school district and parents) that groupwork as a vehicle for teaching and learning is legitimate and effective, and therefore worthy of an investment of effort and resources.

Because groupwork is a demanding pedagogy and an uncertain enterprise, teachers, like their students, benefit from opportunities to work with and learn from colleagues. Such opportunities arise when professional developers "walk the talk" (see Case 15). For teachers to understand the intricacies of groupwork as a classroom strategy and to develop professional judgment and decision making to respond to its inherent uncertainty, professional development needs to be more than the presentation of models to be implemented mechanistically (see Cases 3, 8, and 10). Furthermore, as with groups of students, status problems emerge and need to be addressed in adult groups as well. For instance, in Case 15, the teacher–author expresses this disappointment: "Adults who train young students on the benefits of groupwork couldn't function as group members in a training session. We are in charge of treating status problems in the classroom and we can't even fix our own. Intervening and trying to treat the problem was seen by Jerry as exacerbating it. When he prevented me from trying to fix the problem, he gave me the impression that if we didn't do anything it would magically disappear. I wonder what Jerry does in his class when these types of problems crop up. Does he tell the students to be quiet and that the problem will go away if [they] don't talk about it or confront it?"

Successful implementation also depends on regular and systematic follow-up in the classroom by experts (staff developers, supportive coaches) and by sustained conversations among colleagues. Beyond discussions of the successes or difficulties of individual students as group members, such conversations need to focus on substantive issues and dilemmas of curriculum and instruction in groupwork.

Finally, parents are the "extra audience" (see Case 14) whom teachers and administrators need to inform of the merits of groupwork. Without that, this "extra audience" can undermine a teacher's sense of efficacy. For instance, after receiving the letter of the parent who called the groupwork assignment "fluff" and "crap," the teacher describes her reaction: "With one fell swoop, that letter wiped out all the satisfaction I felt about the Living Art project. I was shocked at its angry, sarcastic tone, thinking I must have done something dreadfully wrong to elicit such a scathing response from a parent. Sara happens to be one of my strongest students, and I thought we had a good relationship. After reading her father's letter, I completely reevaluated our relationship. Understandably, the letter also caused me to rethink the Living Art assignment and groupwork in general."

CONCLUSION: WE'RE ALL IN THIS TOGETHER

In the last case of this volume, the teacher–author describes her journey of learning to use groupwork. Her description touches on many of the issues we have posited. What we have done in an expository mode in this introduction the author does in a narrative literary mode. In our experience using these cases in pre-service and in-service contexts, the combination of theoretical exposition and discussions of teacher–authored narratives resonates deeply with practitioners. The cases in this book illuminate many intertwined dilemmas of groupwork. The teachers with whom we have worked have found these narratives to be provocative companions on their own journeys. Now, as you turn to the cases in this volume, we hope they touch your imagination and guide your "odyssey" as well.

REFERENCES

Cohen, E. G. (1994a). *Designing groupwork: Strategies for heterogeneous classrooms* (2nd ed.). New York: Teachers College Press.

Cohen, E. G. (1994b). *Status treatments for the classroom* [Video]. New York: Teachers College Press.

Cohen, E. G. (1994c). Restructuring the classroom: Conditions for productive small groups. *Review of Educational Research, 64*, 1–35.

Cohen, E. G., & Lotan, R. A. (1995). Producing equal-status interaction in the heterogeneous classroom. *American Educational Research Journal, 32*, 99–120.

Cohen, E. G., & Lotan, R. A. (1997). *Working for equity in heterogeneous classrooms: Sociological theory in practice.* New York: Teachers College Press.

Cohen, E. G., Lotan, R. A., & Catanzarite, L. (1990). Treating status problems in the cooperative classroom. In S. Sharan (Ed.), *Cooperative learning: Theory and research* (pp. 203–229). New York: Praeger.

Cohen, E. G., Lotan, R. A., & Holthuis, N. (1995). Talking and working together: Conditions for learning in complex instruction. In M. T. Hallinan (Ed.), *Restructuring schools: Promising practices and policies* (pp. 157–174). New York: Plenum Press.

Cohen, E. G., Lotan, R. A., with Leechor, C. (1989). Can classrooms learn? *Sociology of Education, 62*, 75—94.

Ehrlich, D., & Zack, M. (1997). The power in playing the part. In E. G. Cohen & R. A. Lotan (Eds.), *Working for equity in heterogeneous classrooms: Sociological theory in practice.* New York: Teachers College Press.

Gardner, H. (1983). *Frames of mind.* New York: Basic Books.

Johnson, D. W., & Johnson, R. T. (1994). *Learning together and alone: Cooperative, competitive, and individualistic learning* (4th ed.). Englewood Cliffs, NJ: Prentice Hall.

Lotan, R. (1997). Principles of a principled curriculum. In E. G. Cohen & R. A. Lotan (Eds.), *Working for equity in heterogeneous classrooms: Sociological theory in practice.* New York: Teachers College Press.

Qin, Z., Johnson, D. W., & Johnson, R. T. (1995). Cooperative versus competitive efforts and problem solving. *Review of Educational Research, 65*(2), 129–143.

Sharan, S. (1994). *Handbook of cooperative learning methods.* Westport, CT: Greenwood Press.

Slavin, R. (1990). *Cooperative learning: Theory, research, and practice.* Englewood Cliffs, NJ: Prentice Hall.

Webb, N. (1995). Group collaboration in assessment: Multiple objectives, processes, and outcomes. *Educational Evaluation and Policy Analysis, 17*(2), 239–261.

CHAPTER 1

Conceptions of Teaching and Learning

Introducing new ideas and supporting student learning is a challenging endeavor under any circumstances. But when teachers try to incorporate groupwork into their instruction and encourage students to teach and learn from one another, their conceptions of teaching and learning must become much more complex than traditional whole-class approaches. Suddenly, certain issues become more prominent: how to develop classroom community and norms for collaboration; how to motivate students to assume some responsibility for their own learning; how to redefine the role of teacher as a facilitator of learning rather than merely a transmitter of information; how to assess learning; and how to manage the classroom. All of the cases in this chapter are situated in instructional episodes and address these issues.

Case 1

When Do You Intervene?

My personal and professional experience have taught me that people don't hear something until they are ready. As a veteran teacher, I know this is true for my students as well. Yet all too often I find myself trying to give them the "right answer"—as if there were one. In recent years I've tried to break myself of this habit; however, this has been problematic.

I teach fifth and sixth grade in an inner-city school where for the last three years I have participated in a research project (Fostering a Community of Learners) designed by Ann Brown and Joe Campione from the University of California, Berkeley. The thrust of the program, which entails extensive restructuring of many aspects of the daily curricula, is to create a classroom where students engage in their own research in the field of biological sciences. The project's ultimate goal is for students to become literate in a number of areas, including reading, writing, argumentation, and the discourse of science.

As a result of the restructuring, there has been a blending of whole-class work and groupwork, in which students do collaborative research projects in small groups. During small group sessions, students do research, participate in Reciprocal Teaching,* and work on writing a group paper about their research findings. Once the research is complete, the groups re-form into a jigsaw configuration.** This exciting role reversal presents the adult facilitator with an interesting question—what to do when one of the students, in his or her role as teacher, presents incorrect information? Should there be some sort of intervention? When and how?

I had to answer these questions for myself this year when my students undertook a research project about the island of Borneo. To begin the project, I presented the students with a true story about a serious outbreak of malaria on the island: after many people died, authorities had decided to spray DDT to kill the mosquitoes carrying the malaria. What they hadn't anticipated was DDT's effect on the ecosystem.

My students were challenged first to uncover and understand the complexities of the Borneo dilemma and then to consider possible solutions. Once familiar with the elements that contributed to this dilemma, the students generated a number of questions about the situation. The questions served as a springboard from which individual research groups designed their own research projects. Each group investigated individual topics, among them: What is DDT? Why did this island's rulers decide to use it? What is malaria? What, if any, ethical issues were (or should have been) considered in the decision to use a pesticide?

After completing their research, all students participated in a final jigsaw session. Each student adopted the attitude of someone having the "right" information, presenting the newly acquired knowledge with conviction. Yet as experts emerge in a new domain, these students' newly formed theories are sometimes erroneous. As the classroom teacher, my responsibility is to decide when it is important to inject correct information. In this case the issue first arose with Lakesha.

---

* Reciprocal Teaching (RT) was designed by Ann Marie Palincsar and Ann Brown in 1984. RT provides students with a set of cognitive strategies which enable the reader to have greater access and understanding of the text. Through a variety of questions, first modeled by an adult, the child learns the importance of clarifying, predicting, summarizing and interpreting newly revealed material. After seeing strategies modeled by an adult, students are encouraged to take turns being the "teacher." Eventually all RT groups are directed by the students.

**Jigsaw configurations, a model of groupwork developed by Elliot Aronson, has two stages. In a typical classroom, the teacher divides the students into approximately five groups. During the first stage, the teacher assigns each group a specific topic about which the members will become expert; the group conducts research or discusses the topic and ensures that all members understand the material. During the second stage, the teacher reconfigures the groups so that each newly formed group has one expert on each of the topics; the experts share their knowledge with the others so that all have a deep understanding of the material.

Lakesha's group had researched general information about the island of Borneo, and she was deemed the resident expert. Everything the other students would learn about the island was to come from her, and like all the other students, she took this heady responsibility very seriously.

A fellow student, Ugochi, asked, "Is Borneo like New York?" "Yes," Lakesha responded, "it is just like New York, but it has more trees."

This was a significant error. In this lesson the students were supposed to understand that the people of Borneo made widespread use of DDT because of a serious malaria outbreak, and one of the reasons malaria was so widespread was that Borneo is a tropical country. New York City's significantly different climate makes it less likely that malaria would be a problem there.

When I heard Lakesha's answer, I considered whether to intervene. On one hand, I wondered: if the students didn't understand that Borneo's vast swampy areas had led to the increased incidence of malaria, how could they understand why the government had agreed to spray DDT? On the other hand, I thought: Lakesha was a very low-status child. If I corrected her during her presentation, would she retain her power in the group as the "expert"? I decided not to intervene.

That evening I discussed the incident with a colleague, one of the program's designers. We agreed that this situation was problematic. Sometimes incorrect information can have broader ramifications, confusing students as they try to come to new understanding about complex situations. Moreover, our project is not about unbridled discovery learning. We want students to have a sound science framework and a deep understanding of certain important biological concepts.

During our discussion, my colleague reminded me of the importance of what she calls "opportunistic seeding"—waiting for the right moment to drop some pearls of wisdom, with the understanding that we hear only what we are ready to hear. Rather than intervene directly to correct Lakesha's mistake, I decided to wait for an opportune moment to drop a seed that might lead students to understand Borneo is a tropical place.

I didn't have to wait long. The next jigsaw session topic was on malaria. Emecia, the student expert, began her talk by saying that in order to grow malaria you needed a wet, swampy place. Seeing my chance, I raised my hand. When Emecia called on me, I said, "I am confused. Yesterday Lakesha said Borneo was like New York City, and I don't think of New York City as swampy. So how can malaria be a problem?" Lakesha immediately took the bait, saying, "You misunderstood me. Only part of Borneo is like New York—the cities."

At this point Ugochi chimed in, "Yeah, don't you remember? Borneo has tropical rain forests, too. That's where the swampy areas are."

This started a lively discussion about the terrain of Borneo and why it's conducive to the spread of malaria. The students looked at me in amazement, wondering how I could have missed this most salient of points. But I smiled smugly to myself, feeling as if all was right with the world—until the next day, when Doranne presented as the expert on DDT.

During her presentation, Doranne was asked to clarify a point in her paper. She had written that DDT "was more dangerous for children because it gets in their bodies and then it continues to grow as [the children] get bigger and bigger. The bigger the child gets, the more DDT it has in [its] system."

"Oh, no," I thought. This was a potentially serious misunderstanding. Once again I had to make a quick decision to intervene or not. Should I set this kid straight, or wait and deal with it in a whole class lesson after the jigsaw? Because I felt that Doranne was very self-confident, I decided to question her about her conjecture.

I said, "It is my understanding that DDT is a pesticide, a nonliving thing. I think there is a characteristic missing for it to be able to grow. What is that?" After some discussion, we concluded that in order for something to grow, that something must be alive. So I asked Doranne, "Is DDT alive?"

When she said no, I pressed further, asking, "Then how does a child get more DDT into his system?" Doranne explained that initially a child might eat a fruit or vegetable that has been sprayed with DDT. After that, the DDT gets in the body and it grows.

At this point I fell back into my old teacher stance, continuing to debate this point in hopes that Doranne would give in. But she held her ground, refusing to be swayed by the logic of my argument.

Not only did Doranne remain unconvinced, but the jigsaw session, which had only moments before been child centered, was now focused totally on my input. Everyone was looking at me to see what wisdom I had to impart, trying to understand my "right" way of thinking. The students had been looking at each other, building a learning community among themselves and enjoying each other's intellectual company; now I was the center of attention, with little or nothing to show for it.

When I realized what had happened, I tried to give the floor back to the students by asking the next child to present. I backed off physically, making it clear that I was still listening, but trying to shift the focus of attention back to the students.

The focus did shift. But as I continued to observe, I realized that Doranne, the child I had tried to correct, never spoke again during that jigsaw session. I was reminded of—in fact, haunted by—something I had read in Courtney Cazden's book *Classroom Discourse* (1988), when she challenges the traditional role of the teacher: "Teachers have the right to speak at any time

and to any person; they can fill any silence or interrupt any speaker; they can speak to a student anywhere in the room and in any volume or tone of voice" (p. 54). Had I overextended my power as the teacher to the detriment of that child?

What should I have done? I still don't know. Clearly there are no easy answers. In one instance, intervention helped. In the other, it hindered.

When I initially changed my classroom to accommodate groupwork, I talked with my students about how this would increase their independence and responsibility. We discussed how everyone would become an expert as we built a community that valued the sharing of knowledge. Those were lofty notions. But how can we bring our highest and best ideas into the classroom while at the same time safeguarding educational and intellectual integrity?

REFERENCE

Cazden, C. B. (1988). *Classroom discourse: The language of teaching and learning.* Portsmouth, NH: Heinemann Press.

Case 2

Groupwork? Rats!

Six second grade students stood around a rectangular library table covered with butcher paper. It was their turn to get a close look at our classroom rat, Popsicle, and maybe even pet her. As part of a year-long study of animals, their task for the next 10 minutes was to observe the rat, watch her movements, and mark with an "X" wherever she stopped on the table. Next, they would describe her movements or draw her in their logs. I reviewed the guidelines and took the rat out of the cage.

As I started to leave, Michelle asked if they could hold the rat. I replied, "Not this time. Wait until you're recording in your logs. You can take turns holding her while you write. For now, just watch and map how she moves. You can call her and tap gently on the table. You can coax her to follow a pencil." I then walked away to check in with the other four groups.

The group, formed by random selection, started out quietly, members standing side by side around their table. No one wanted the rat to go over the edge. I heard:

"Make an 'X' there."
"She's not coming to my end."
"Quit hitting the table."
"She's scared."

After a few minutes, Popsicle lingered at one end of the table. The whole group crowded there except for John, who had become a self-appointed organizer. John circled the table, saying in a loud voice, "We need some here and here and here." He kept reminding the others that someone should stand near the opposite end because the rat moved fast. Terrell went to the other end briefly, but quickly returned, crowding into the place he'd left. A minute later Michelle picked up Popsicle, cradling the rat in her arms. But when a dropping fell, she screamed. Lisa giggled and backed up, pushing Joshua.

"See?" John yelled. "You weren't supposed to pick her up."

Pointing toward the rat dropping, Lauren goaded Michelle, saying, "You should make an 'X' there." Michelle hit her.

When Terrell picked up the rat and held it in front of Lauren's face, John yelled, "You aren't being respectful." The rat squirmed away from Terrell.

It was the last straw for a group on the edge of chaos. The room, always too noisy with kids' voices bouncing from the wooden walls and rafters, teetered toward disorder. I walked over to the table, scooped up Popsicle, and put her in the cage. I took the butcher paper off and told the group to put their heads down, hoping everyone would cool off. They sat with their heads down for the next 10 minutes while I went around helping the other groups. But I kept an authoritarian teacher's eye on them, as well as on the other groups.

After 16 years as a primary teacher, I had started this school year in a new role—as a science specialty teacher for 350 students in grades one to five at an inner-city elementary school. Eighty percent of the students are African American; the others are Hispanic, Filipino, Iranian, Southeast Asian, and Caucasian. I wondered how I was ever going to learn their names, much less facilitate learning the scientific method in a "science lab." To try to know them better, I used student surveys.

Throughout the year, two questions framed my teaching. How does a community of learners develop for students working in groups with hands-on activities for the first time? How can predictable processes be established to support positive study habits when students meet twice a week for 50-minute periods in "science lab"? By midyear, three routines helped to make a sense of community:

1. <u>Community building activities</u>. Classes started or ended with community building activities, such as a community circle. Children sat in a circle for a structured sharing and listening activity. The sharing was brief. It focused on a specific topic. Sometimes the topic related to science, but often we shared weekend activities, favorites, and other opinions.

2. <u>Rotating work stations</u>. Gradually I developed a protocol for rotating stations. Children worked each semester in randomly selected fixed groups. Some stations were related—for example, observing our rat, answering class-generated questions about it, and writing and creating a page for a pop-up rat book. At another station students explored the volume of various containers to get ready for a lesson about density. At the "Changes" stations, students observed and recorded the changes in plants, a classroom compost box, a beaker of water, and various crystals. Every third or fourth time we met, I guided a whole group activity to set up for the "Changes" station, or I gave them a directed lesson.

3. <u>Writing in learning logs</u>. Students worked, observed, and explored while recording in logs. At the end of each class, the log entries were shared.

Each group had a new leader twice a month who passed out materials, initiated the work process, and reported the group's progress at the end of each session. Sometimes they worked as individuals at the same table, sometimes as partners, sometimes in two subgroups of three, and sometimes on a table group activity.

In this particular project, I wanted the group to discover that observation and interaction lead to authentic learning. I hoped that by working together to map the rat's movements, the students would look more closely at the variety of rat movements and begin to speculate together on the rat's abilities. I wanted to promote and honor students' ability to find their own way to work together. Because of this, I hadn't rushed over at once when I'd seen the first signs of difficulty.

After I finally intervened, I wondered if I shouldn't have first processed the flare-up both for the group and the class. But the other tables had quickly reengaged in their tasks and seemed to want to complete their work. Or maybe they just wanted to disassociate themselves from the rat group.

Hindsight tells me it's not surprising that working together to map out the rat's movement had produced anxiety in John. He struggles through school and says he does his best work when sitting by himself. Perhaps his anxiety set off the rest of the group, which, as the first group to do this particular activity, was already a little insecure.

Did stressing the importance of their working together to produce the map affect them negatively? I considered spending a period preparing the students to map the rat's movements. But in my rush to get to the activity, we spent only a few minutes practicing their social strategies. After all, they had cooperated during a prior animal observation task in which they'd looked at the rat together, talked to each other, then individually recorded observations in their logs. A quick look at some of those earlier log entries reveals that the group had been cooperative and engaged in their observation:

It scratched me. (John)

Popsicle the rat. Popsicle is a white rat. Popsicle likes Michelle. Popsicle is looking at me. Popsicle likes to play. (Lauren)

He is sniffing and he is standing up. He was sniffing on my book. He has red eyes. His claws were on my book. (Jamal)

Popsicle is an albino rat. That means he has red eyes. He tried to go off the table sometimes. If you put your pencil high in the air, he will stand up. When the teacher got him out of the cage, his tail was spinning around like a helicopter. (Lisa)

Their next group task closely mirrored the kind of work they routinely did in their classrooms: looking up answers to questions in a book. From a list of class questions about rats which were student generated, the group selected three to five questions to answer as a group. Each pair of students used a different resource—books or a poster chart. They had to all agree on the answer to the question based on their previous observations, classroom instruction, and resource material. Next they were to help each other write in their logs. I asked them to focus on their work together, not on the number of questions they could answer in their logs. I went as far as saying I expected them to be working on the same question.

I thought this assignment seemed dull compared to the hands-on activities at the other tables, but the group nodded and grabbed their pencils. Lisa, an accomplished reader, quickly began to lead them through the questions. At first, Michelle and John, easily frustrated with the discussion, asked me for the right answer. I reminded them that I wouldn't help until each pair had looked through their resources, the group agreed they needed help, and everyone raised their hands together. They no longer asked. Somehow it became a challenge to find the answer as a group.

Whenever I checked in, they were working. They read aloud the first question and passages from their books. They informally jigsawed and worked in pairs on the next two questions. They excitedly called the other pairs over when they found information to back up their ideas. Individuals occasionally strayed from the task, just talking, but they all returned to their work.

It's true that not everyone engaged to the same degree in this activity. Mia and John participated marginally in the discussion and worked intermittently with their partners, looking through their book. They copied the answers while the others composed and discussed spelling as a group. Yet the group's assessment of themselves at the end shows they felt they had all worked together and done a good job.

Like the students, I was pleased to see half a page of questions and answers written in their logs, a measurable accomplishment for second graders, who often like to quantify their work. Yet I wanted them to value not just quantity of output, but their own process. So I reminded them and the rest of the class that these were questions that *they* had asked about rats. I told them they had been thinking, investigating, and observing the animals' activities in the classroom, just like scientists.

Did students consider their work good in this task because the question-answer activity was familiar? Did they, like me, struggle with factoring in the level of difficulty when assessing the success or failure of an assignment? The question-answer activity was simple, with a measurable product to assess. By contrast, the rat mapping activity had demanded more attention, self-control, and cooperation, and success would have been less quantifiable. Log recordings would have provided just a peek at the knowledge the students gained from their observations and interactions with each other. How do students consider complexity when assessing their work?

Now, after seven months in my new role, I still have many questions. The process and the outcomes of the two group episodes I described echoed the larger dilemmas that I struggled with throughout the year. The room was quieter and more orderly with large group instruction. Students called the more traditional reading and question-answer activities "real learning." Hands-on groupwork often required interaction that sent the room through increasingly uncomfortable noise levels amplified by the wooden ceiling and walls, threatening classroom order. Students didn't associate groupwork—even when successful—with real learning. I wonder if students feel less secure generating their own questions and finding answers from multiple resources than they are working with questions and "real" answers from a textbook. What can I do to expand their concept of "real learning"?

I also struggle with the 50-minute period and groupwork organization. Are rotating learning stations the best structure, considering time constraints? How much time should I devote to modeling and practicing group process and problem solving strategies? As a teacher I want to construct some kind of rhythm to the day that meshes with my coaching style of teaching. Whole-class activities in each session seem like isolated experiences, with me having to orchestrate the links between them. Working in stations, in contrast, gives students a preview of their next task, a chance to revisit an activity through sharing student work, and a sense of familiarity as station activities are gradually modified. But I rarely squeeze in periods for modeling and practicing social strategies and group problem solving techniques. Do I need to spend more time for these kinds of lessons? Is my program of working in stations too ambitious, too complicated? Will the students see the work they do in stations as both learning and fun? Would a more direct instructional approach that includes whole-class hands-on activities be more effective than using rotation exclusively?

Case 3

Poor Period 3!

I stand at my classroom door to greet my students. Soon period 3 will begin. "Good morning, Latisha, how are you?"

"What are we doing today?" she responds.

I try not to sound too mechanical. "I'll explain to everyone in class at once, Latisha." She plops into her seat and stares; her need for nurturing goes unmet.

"Hi, Jose, what's up?"

"I hate my group," he says. "Let me sit near Donny."

"That's not negotiable, Jose." Noticing my robot tone, I add, "You'll have to work with all kinds of people in this world and here's the place to learn!" I see pouting, and again, pressing needs not being met.

Period 3 is one of six eighth grade social studies classes I teach each day. We cover U.S. history, government, and geography. Our school draws from what is largely a lower-middle-class neighborhood with an ethnically diverse population, and the majority are Latino. Two-and-a-half years ago, I became an advocate of cooperative group learning. Especially for our large "sheltered" population (i.e., English language learners), it seemed to me group interaction would be preferable to students' struggling alone in silence. During my conversion to groupwork, I was trained never to give up—if things aren't working out, keep discussing it with the class until they cooperate. Because of my relative success with instruction in cooperative groups, I'd been selected to be a peer coach, observing and helping other teachers to plan, manage, and evaluate their groupwork.

Thus, feeling a little smug, I entered into group instruction this year with a good deal of confidence. I met my match with period 3. In my mind I call them "poor period 3." This is one class in the district that merits a full time Resource Specialist Program teaching aide because we have nine—yes, nine—special education students. We also have 10 sheltered students who have recently left bilingual classes and are now making the transition to full-time English instruction. The makeup of this class creates a disturbing chemistry that is felt within 30 seconds of the starting bell. I usually place them in groups of four or five, then invariably watch in frozen amazement as they torment each other. I persist as I was trained to do, but find myself wondering whether groupwork is appropriate for this uncooperative class of 28 students, skewed with a disproportionate number of emotionally needy individuals.

That question loomed especially large one day when we were reviewing the exploration and colonial settlement of the United States. To show how hard it was for early settlements to survive in the New World, I chose a group activity called *Elementary Eagle*. In the context of this lesson, the *Elementary Eagle* is a ship that has just crossed the Atlantic Ocean—in approximately 1604—and landed along the coast near what is today the James River in Virginia.

Before the students break into groups, we discuss some strategies the Colonists used to stay alive, such as trading with the Native Americans. At this point, a student whom I refer to as "Mr. Impossible" (because he does not belong in a regular classroom by any stretch of the most patient teacher's imagination) starts to mimic Mr. Rogers on TV. "I'm going to be your har-r-monizer today, group," he quips, following the remark with a phony, exaggerated grin. As is common with Mr. Impossible, he chooses an inopportune moment to interrupt—just when I have all of the students somewhat focused, the moment when I'm ready to switch tracks and say those magic words: "You are now in your groups!" Today, I say them anyway, quickly, before another student, who I call "It's-Not-My-Fault-Walt," can chime in, as he is prone to do. This year Walt receives no extra support from our school district because his test scores are too low for special education and too high for the mentally retarded classes. Walt is as low-status as you can get.

Once the groups are under way, I notice that Walt is on task—at least initially. Each member of the group reads a role—fisherman, farmer, carpenter, merchant, or soldier. As a group they are supposed to study the map provided and decide on the best place to settle and survive in the new land. But after reading his role, Walt loses interest and leaves his group to distract someone in another group.

"Walt, there is no interaction between groups," I say. "We've been over the group ground rules several times."

"But we were just talking about the work," pleads It's-Not-My-Fault-Walt.

"What about the work, Walt?" I ask, even as I realize that he's hooked me.

"Can we leave early for lunch?" is his response.

"Only the facilitator in the group is allowed to ask the teacher questions, Walt," I reply, with yet another of my clinical answers. I then wonder if anyone in Walt's group understands the task, and I ask Grace if she is the group facilitator today. Grace, who in many ways fits her name and is probably the most responsible student in the class, tries valiantly to recenter the group. But she doesn't handle leadership roles easily. I suggest that other students in the group can help clarify the directions. At last they understand. Stan says, "You represent the view of the role you read, then we draw an X on the map on the spot where the group decides is the best place to settle. As a group we will present our reasons for our choice to the other groups and be prepared for them to challenge our reasoning."

In other classes this activity has usually turned out to be fun. Equally important, it stimulates higher-level thinking skills. But not so in period 3. As you may have predicted, we have to "batten down the hatches." We nearly avoid a simulation of World War III, with name-calling as the first-strike weapon. The more explosive personalities don't want to wait their turns. Mr. Impossible continues, announcing with a false grin, "I'm the ha-a-r-r-monizer." And the disinterested girls gravitate together to thumb through *Tiger Beat* magazine.

After nearly an entire period of ineffective groupwork, I spend the closing minutes of class, as I have been coached, debriefing period 3 about why things are or are not working well. In this case, since they are not working well, we talk about how we can get them to work better. Because the students' stomachs begin to grumble for lunch, they try to pacify me with what they think I want to hear, answers they've read and now repeat from signs that are up in my classroom most of the year. We discuss what you can do if the facilitator in your group doesn't take charge, and we also role play positive body language to better understand its positive effects on the group members. When the role playing is met with a civil reaction, I see a glimmer of hope!

I dismiss students for lunch by groups, with the students who have cooperated most effectively leaving first. Usually a good strategy, in this case it results in name-calling among members of those groups dismissed last.

To sum it up, after 42 minutes with period 3, I feel like a giant, emotion-filled ball being slammed from one side of the room to the other. There are just too many emotions flying around the room and rebounding off the walls. Whether it's because they lack experience in small group interaction or they lack self-esteem, or some combination of the two, creating a cooperative atmosphere is not something the students of period 3 seem able to accomplish.

At the end of the day I find myself wondering why I don't switch to the more traditional teacher-controlled setting with which these students are more familiar. Perhaps groupwork is not meant for *every* class. "It's okay to give up," I tell myself. Yet deep down I tell myself, "It's *not* okay." I know I need to do *something*.

It's been several weeks since this episode and I notice some positive changes. I started with a compromise, opting to limit groupwork to one day a week. Then I sought and received helpful advice from the other four teachers in our Interdisciplinary Team. But the best move I made was to attend the after-school football games.

Seven members of my third period are on the team, and each seemed both surprised and pleased to see that I cared enough to come to the games. They appreciated the individual attention that groupwork does not seem to provide for them. I felt that it was important to see them in a context in which they are successful because so often they seem uncomfortable in our classroom setting.

Back in class I praised them for their cooperation in sports and wove this experience into groupwork at effective moments. Since my visits to the football games, my discipline problems have been cut in half. In retrospect I realize that many of my students in period 3 need an entire rooting section just for themselves in order to relax and learn in a group. I have also noticed a change since we took our field trip to Superior Court to see a real trial, followed by lunch at the pizza parlor. Seeing each other in a different situation—not sitting in chairs at desks—gives teacher and students a different perspective and appreciation of one another. There is a little less tension now.

I have also arranged for a "holding pen" for Mr. Impossible, another supervised room where I can send him before he becomes too exasperating. Mr. Impossible is currently undergoing neurological testing. Meanwhile,

It's-Not-My-Fault-Walt is being interviewed to qualify for some kind of support from the district.

Time also creates trust, which had been the missing ingredient. I am grateful too that I have been blessed with an easygoing nature, and most of all, that I have managed to maintain a positive attitude. You have to! There is no choice. My goal is for these students to feel we are all on the *same* team and to understand that developing good group skills is more valuable than knowing which branch of government is granted the "elastic clause" or being able to regurgitate the contents of the Wilmot Proviso. I want them to understand that getting along is more valued than resistance.

"Time and trust," I whisper to myself every day at noon, as I see them off. Then I sit down and eat my lunch, refueling for the "angels" in my afternoon classes.

Case 4

Do You Let Kids Fail?

During seven years of teaching chemistry, I have been surprised and disappointed at the extent to which students depend on me to confirm their ideas and to acknowledge that they are somehow correct or right. They are locked into learning the right answer, are often unable to adequately debate an opinion in contrast to their own, and seem totally unaware of the importance of the problem solving process. Most students define learning as knowing a collection of right answers. This differs significantly from my own high school experience.

I teach chemistry at a public high school that has some of the richest and poorest students in the San Francisco Bay Area. Approximately 50 ethnic groups are represented by our students, and my chemistry classes are an excellent reflection of the school's ethnic and academic diversity.

I went to a high school with a completely self-paced, self-motivated, independent learning program. I was allowed complete freedom in planning and implementing my secondary education. I was able to plan my class schedule on a daily basis, to create a list of requirements to demonstrate that I had learned the material, and to design performance-based criteria for evaluating my proficiency in a specific area.

No doubt influenced by this experience, my philosophy is that students need to take an active role in their education, to be responsible for their learning. They should learn as much from the process of identifying problems, hypothesizing solutions, analyzing the consequences of probable answers, and deciding upon a plan of action as they learn from the final solution.

I have often wondered whether students are limited to their narrow definition of learning because they have never been given an opportunity to experience the process of truly learning something for themselves. This year I decided to see if my students were able to function with more freedom. Using a cooperative learning teaching strategy called Complex Instruction,* I decided to provide my students with an opportunity to experience for themselves the discovery of learning— and of teaching.

The Complex Instruction model focuses on student-centered activities and emphasizes the dynamics of working cooperatively to solve problems. To ensure participation by all members of the group, each student performs a specific role. Students are responsible not just for their own growth, but for the learning of the group. Prior to beginning the Complex Instruction curriculum, students develop and practice interpersonal skills using mini-activities called "skillbuilders." Skillbuilders require students to complete a highly interdependent task and provide them with the opportunity to develop strategies for working with others.

During the first month of school, I used skillbuilders with all of my classes and felt students were adequately prepared to function in a group before assigning a Complex Instruction curriculum unit. On average, my students participated in a Complex Instruction unit once a month.

In February, after the students had completed four Complex Instruction units, I developed a unit to examine the behavior of gases. Each student group of four selected a portion of material presented in a unit on gases. The student groups were to investigate the effects of concentration, temperature, and pressure on the behavior of gases. In essence, the groups would research the topic and become instructors for the class for that aspect of the unit.

To ensure the completeness of the teaching assignment, within each group, each student performed a dual role. The roles were: facilitator and presentation specialist,

---

* Complex Instruction, developed at Stanford University, is a groupwork model that emphasizes the development of higher-order thinking skills in heterogeneous classrooms. It addresses issues of status that arise in small groups.

reporter and homework specialist, encourager and evaluation specialist, and materials and equipment specialist. The students in each group learned the material, organized the information, planned a creative lesson, presented that lesson, designed a homework assignment, and then evaluated their peers' understanding of the material. In essence, they were the teachers for the unit.

My role was facilitator, or coach, for the groups. I recommended additional research material, suggested sources for supplies, and listened to each group's plan of action. When group members asked me to validate their ideas, I responded by asking questions for them to reflect upon.

The groups were evaluated by me and by four randomly selected classmates, using criteria designed by the class as a whole (see Figure 4.1, the peer evaluation form). After some discussion, the class agreed that the 25-minute presentations would be evaluated according to how well they followed the ground rules:

1. no more than five minutes of direct instruction (lecture);

2. the presentation required the use of a demo, lab, skit, or game to provide interactive learning;

3. visual props or musical highlights were required; and

4. all members of the group would participate in the teaching process.

The entire class would ultimately need to understand the information presented, and students were relying on each other as instructors.

Students used two 50-minute class periods to prepare their lesson plans. During that time they met with me for approximately 15 minutes to discuss their presentation outlines.

Reactions to this assignment were as diverse as the student body. Some groups were very confident about their newly acquired knowledge and eager to teach the class. Others were in a panic and had already decided that their presentation would be a complete failure.

One group simply said, "Tell us what you want the class to learn and we will give it our best shot." Appalled at their attitude, I explained, "*You* are the teachers. You get to decide what the class should learn and how to present the information to your peers." "But how do you begin something like this?" asked Sarah, the facilitator. Determined not to buy into their helplessness, I decided to answer every question with another question, unless safety was at stake. In this instance I asked Sarah, "What piece or pieces of information are the most important in your section?" The group members responded with facial expressions that would have intimidated a novice teacher. Ignoring the body language, I continued: "If you were limited to writing one sentence about this section of the text, what would it be? I suggest you write the sentence after you have discussed it, and I'll be back in a few minutes to see how you're doing." I could hear sounds of discontentment, but I was determined that this group was going to stand on its own feet. I was not going to come to the rescue.

When I returned to the group, it was evident that at least two members had a good feeling for the main points of the section. I overheard them telling the rest of the group that it would be important to discuss the definition of pressure and to show how pressure is measured. But though the students appeared to grasp the subject matter, the group wasn't making progress toward completing the task.

I began to analyze the dynamics of this particular foursome. I had selected heterogeneous groups in terms of sex, age, academic performance, social status, and ethnicity. In assigning them, I had also considered students' various learning styles. So why was this group not working?

Do You Let Kids Fail?

Figure 4.1

Peer Evaluation Form—Gas Law Presentations

TITLE OF PRESENTATION: _____

NAMES OF GROUP MEMBERS: _____   _____

_____   _____

CONTENT NOTES:

QUESTIONS OR COMMENTS:

EVALUATION: Each category should be evaluated on a scale of 1 to 5, where 1 is poor and 5 is excellent. Please feel free to write in any additional comments.

1. Apparent knowledge of the topic   _____

2. Appropriate use of a demo, lab, skit, or game   _____

3. Use of visual props or musical highlights   _____

4. Ability of the group to answer questions   _____

5. Participation of the entire group   _____

TOTAL _____

Evaluator's Signature _____   Date _____

Sarah raised her hand, indicating that my presence was needed at her group. As I approached, I reminded myself, "Answer every question with a question." But before she could ask her question, Roger blurted out, "You can't expect us to understand this stuff. That's why they hired *you* to be the teacher." I knew I needed to address Roger's frustration and try to get the group back on task. With the whole class waiting to see how I would respond, I quietly said, "Roger, I appreciate the fact that you are frustrated and I know you want to be successful on this assignment. I am very concerned that your group has been unable to complete this task. Can you identify what the problem seems to be?"

No one responded. There was complete silence. I had anticipated that everyone would blame everyone else and was amazed by the silence. "Please explore the question and I'll be back in a few minutes," I told them as I walked away. But a few minutes later the bell rang and they all left without a word.

The group was to make its presentation the next day, and as far as I could tell, they had no plan. What would happen the next day? This group was convinced that I was responsible for their learning and that I would rescue them, that I wouldn't allow them to fail.

So I was faced with the dilemma of my professional life: should I let them fail? Teaching is my chosen profession; I am an excellent teacher and I believe my function as a teacher is to help students become independent, critically thinking, lifelong learners. Yet these students didn't appear interested in learning; they simply wanted to be spoonfed. Give them a list of facts or pieces of information and they would retain it long enough to regurgitate it back to me. How could I convince them that the process of learning and being responsible for one's own learning is more important than some irrelevant collection of facts?

I was up most of the night wondering what I would do when this group failed in front of the class. I wanted to believe that these students had planned to get together on their own time and that they would pull it off the next day. But I wasn't convinced.

The next day, the first group introduced the effects of temperature on a gas and performed a demonstration to prove that when gas molecules are heated they speed up, increase the frequency of collisions, and create an increase in pressure. As they attached a balloon over the top of a Pyrex flask that was being heated on a hot plate, the whole class held its breath waiting to see if the demo would work. At last the temperature change was sufficient to increase the pressure in the flask and the balloon inflated. Then the group separated the class into teams and played a "what if" game. They concluded their presentation by answering questions and passing out a homework assignment. The whole class clapped as group members took their seats.

After thanking the first group, I asked the class to prepare for the next presentation, which was to be that of my most reluctant group.

Sarah and Roger slowly walked to the front of the class while the other group members refused even to acknowledge that they were in the group. When I asked them to go to the front of the class, they said, "We're not in a group!" Reluctantly, they walked to the front of the room. Sarah started by stating, "Our group was unable to complete the task. We couldn't agree on what was important. Our group didn't work together very well." The students sat with their mouths open as Roger said, "I guess Mrs. Stevens will have to teach this if anybody is going to learn anything about the effect of pressure on gas molecules." All of the students quietly sat in their seats and waited for me to take over and teach the class this group's topic.

It suddenly occurred to me that from the very beginning, this foursome had never intended to give the presentation. I couldn't believe how clever they had been. They just went through the motions of wanting to be successful so I would rescue them when they used the "nonfunctioning group" as their excuse. They were very skilled at manipulating other people to take responsibility for their learning. I wondered what lessons were really being learned in our present school system.

As these thoughts went speeding through my mind, the whole class waited for my response. What was I going to do now? I stood in front of the class and said, "It is very disappointing that the group was unable to teach their lesson today. After we wrap up all the other presentations, I would like the class to discuss what can be done when a group is unable to work together. It will be necessary for everyone to learn the material that would have been covered by this group." Then I asked for the next presentation.

I couldn't believe I hadn't stepped in to teach the lesson. As the next group got started, I kept thinking that for the first time in my career I had actually let a group fail. Had they counted on the fact that I always rescued them? Was I doing the right thing? Was I being unfair to the rest of the class?

I'm still not sure of the answers to those questions. For the last four months, I have been observing how these four individuals react when working in different groups to complete cooperative learning activities. In all instances, the groups in which they are involved perform at a lower level and have difficulties in working cooperatively. By contrast, when lessons are taught in a traditional method, such as lecture or class discussions, these same four students are completely motivated and involved. Why do these students reject the opportunity to assume responsibility for their learning? What will it take to reach them?

It's hard to believe a ten-letter word can cause such anguish to educators in general and account for numerous hours of torment for me. *Evaluation* of groupwork activities raises some real tough questions with many unresolved answers.

I teach chemistry at a public high school that has some of the richest and poorest students in the San Francisco Bay Area. Approximately 50 ethnic groups are represented by our students, and my chemistry classes are an excellent reflection of the school's ethnic and academic diversity.

During my seven years as a teacher, I have tried a number of teaching techniques. In the last two years, I added Complex Instruction* as a major tool in my teaching repertoire. During the first month of school, I taught a unit on the concept of density—typically a difficult idea for students to understand. I created the four-day unit, called the Ups and Downs of Things, using the curriculum design principles of Complex Instruction. My goal was to provide an opportunity for students to discover that all substances have a specific density and that density is the ratio of mass to volume for any substance. On the first day, each group performed a different activity that concentrated on the central question "What is density?" Only I knew the question, however. I had intentionally avoided using the word "density" when I'd introduced the activities. I wanted my students to perform various activities and then hypothesize the central question or idea.

One group had a large bucket and 20 different items. The members hypothesized and stated their rationale for which objects would float and which would sink. Then the group designed and conducted an experiment to test its hypothesis. Finally, the students created a table to illustrate their results.

_____

* Complex Instruction, developed at Stanford University, is a groupwork model that emphasizes the development of higher-order thinking skills in heterogeneous classrooms. It addresses issues of status that arise in small groups.

The second group experimented with four unknown solutions that contained different food coloring. Using a potato and a drinking straw, the members determined how the four liquids could be separated into distinctly different layers. The group tested the liquids and completed a visual display for the class.

A third group read a story about two women hiking in the woods. The women stumble upon a small stream and decide to leave their Coke and Diet Coke cans in the water to keep them cool. When they return, one of the cans is missing. The group had to hypothesize which can was missing and then justify the hypothesis. I provided a large bucket of water and cans of Coke and Diet Coke to assist the group in its exploration. Finally, the group wrote a letter to the two women explaining what had happened.

Another group measured the mass and volume of a number of metal samples. The students used a scale to weigh the samples and used a water displacement method to calculate the volume. After collecting the data, the members plotted the information on a graph and analyzed the relationship between mass and volume.

At the end of the period, students all completed an individual report (see Figure 5.1, individual reports of activities 1–4) responding to a few questions about their specific tasks. The questions were designed to determine if the students understood the activity and could apply the information to a real-life situation.

The second day, we held a "scientific convention" where each group presented its results. The class asked questions about the proposed hypothesis, the experiments, the results presented, and the assumptions made by the investigators. I was exhilarated. My students were actually *doing* science. The class generated a number of questions for each of the groups and discussed how the group might explore the questions. The variety of questions impressed me. One student asked, for instance, "Why did the Diet Coke have a different mass than the regular Coke? The label indicates that they have the same volume and the cans appear to be the same." The answers were equally impressive. "Maybe the Diet Coke has more gas in it than the regular Coke!" responded one student. "I always burp more when I drink Diet Coke." A third student volunteered her opinion, "I think sugar has a larger mass than Nutrasweet. I want the next group to compare the mass of sugar and Nutrasweet when they do the activity. I hope my group gets to do this tomorrow!"

Were these the same students who a few days before had refused to use the term "mass"? What was happening to them? They really wanted to figure out the difference between the Coke and Diet Coke. I would never have imagined that this question would be so engaging for them.

Figure 5.1

Individual Student Reports, Activities 1–4

THE UPS AND DOWNS OF THINGS!!
Key Idea: In what ways do ups & downs of things affect our lives?
Activity #1 What sinks and why?
Individual Report #1

Life jackets are an integral part of boating in the U.S. Even when you rent a paddle boat, you are required to use a life jacket, and when a boat or ship capsizes or a plane goes down at sea, the life jackets are literally life preservers.

1. If you were manufacturing life jackets to be used in an area where the possibility of puncturing an airfilled life jacket is too high, what kind of material would you use, and why would you choose that material over anything else?

2. Why are air or gas filled life jackets the ones most commonly found on aircraft but not so common for activities like pleasure boating or water skiing?

THE UPS AND DOWNS OF THINGS!!
Key Idea: In what ways do ups & downs of things affect our lives?
Activity #2 Creating a rainbow
Individual Report #1

Predict what **you** think will happen to the layers if the straw is turned upside down (with a finger covering the open end of the straw).

Have a group member invert the straw. What was the result? Why do **you** think this happened?

THE UPS AND DOWNS OF THINGS!!
Key Idea: In what ways do ups & downs of things affect our lives?
Activity #3 Don't judge a Coke by its label!
Individual Report #1

Wilma and Margo are still puzzled as to what happened to that can of Coke. Write a letter to them explaining what happened and give them some practical advice when they go backpacking again.

THE UPS AND DOWNS OF THINGS!!
Key Idea: In what ways do ups & downs of things affect our lives?
Activity #4 Is it or is it not, pure gold?
Individual Report #1

Sometimes industry has the need for a material which is a result of two or more elements blended to make an alloy.

What do you hypothesize will be the density of an alloy? Will it be closer to the higher density, the lower density, between, or greater than the higher, or lower than the lowest density?

Test your hypothesis.

On the third day, the groups rotated and performed one of the other activities with the modified questions that had been generated by the class. The fourth day we continued the "scientific convention" to present the conclusions to the newly generated questions.

The activities had been a complete success, and the students were feeling good about how things were going. A few students shared their thoughts in their journal entries. "We should do all of our labs like this," they wrote, and "These activities really helped me understand what's going on in the class." I was thrilled at the responses but I was concerned about the amount of time we had spent on the topic of density. Whereas I would normally spend only one 50-minute period on the topic, I had already spent four class periods. The time commitments for using groupwork had definitely put a strain on my yearly time table, but I was really thrilled that the students were thinking and solving problems in a more meaningful way. Concerned about the curriculum still to be covered, I decided to give a short quiz on density and then continue with the rest of the chapter.

The quiz was traditional in format (see Figure 5.2). It required students to calculate the density of a substance given its mass and volume by rearranging an equation and solving for the unknown variable. It also required them to interpret a data table. It was the same quiz I had always given for density.

I was astonished when I graded the quizzes. These students had not done any better on the test than had students from previous years. I was crushed. I really thought that the students had grasped the concept of density and would be able to apply it. I decided to discuss my disappointment with the students and solicit their input.

The next day I asked, "What did you find difficult about the quiz on density?" The class was unusually quiet. Finally, Marta raised her hand and said, "Our group had a great time doing the activities, and I believe that we had a good understanding of the idea. But the test didn't give us an opportunity to show what we had learned." Everyone was quick to agree with Marta's perspective.

I was still digesting Marta's comments when Carlos raised his hand. This student had never asked a question or raised his hand, so I called upon him immediately. In a very soft voice, Carlos explained: "The quiz was all math. I'm no good in math. I didn't think any of the questions were about the activities we did in class." I thanked the students for their honest responses and asked them to write test questions that they thought would have been more closely related to the activities.

I sat down at my desk, still amazed that the students had not made the connection between the activities and the key ideas of the units. They had participated in the activities and were very attentive when the important issues had come out in the "scientific convention." Two of the groups had actually demonstrated how to derive density from mass and volume data. Yet despite their engagement and attentiveness, they were missing the key concepts. Was there something I should have done to help make the connections more explicit?

At the end of the period, the students turned in their proposed quizzes, which were quite surprising. All of the suggested questions were completely open-ended, and they represented a number of alternatives to evaluate student knowledge. One student suggested a creative story to explain the concept of density. Another would require that a song be written and sung to convey the information about density. A third idea was to take a real-life problem and solve it using the concept of density.

In general, the students selected nontraditional open-ended methods for evaluation. I had never really thought about traditional versus alternative evaluation

Figure 5.2

Two Tests:
Traditional and
Alternative

Chemistry Density Mini Quiz 1

Complete the table using the density equation that was discussed during our scientific convention. You are given two of the variables and asked to solve for the third variable. Please show all of your work in the space provided and include units with your final answers.

Substance	Mass (g)	Volume (ml)	Density (g/ml)
1. NaCl	74.3	27	_____
SHOW WORK:			
2. HCl	_____	96	.36
SHOW WORK:			
3. MgBr^2	72.8	_____	.64
SHOW WORK:			

4. What is the volume, in cubic centimeters, of a sample of cough syrup if it has a mass of 50.0 grams and a density of 0.950 g/cm^3?

5. What is the density of a shiny bar of metal weighing 57.3 grams and having a volume of 4.7 cm^3?

Chemistry Density Mini Quiz 2

Part 1: Use the attached pieces of binder paper to answer this section of the quiz. Select one of the following three alternatives:

1. Write a creative story to explain the concept of density. Imagine you are writing a story for a middle school student.

2. Compose a song that will convey the meaning of density and will explain how density is used in life.

3. Select a real life problem and use your knowledge of density to solve the problem. Explain how you would solve the problem.

Part 2: Please complete all of the problems below. Be sure to show all of your work and include units throughout the problem.

1. How large a container do you need to store 40 grams of a liquid that has a density of 2.0 grams per liter?

2. A copper penny has a mass of 3.1 grams and a volume of 0.35 cm^3. What is the density of copper?

3. A cube is 2 cm on each side. The density of the cube is 10.0 g/cm^3. What is its mass?

before. I had tried to anticipate potential problems when the students had actually performed the activities, but I had not given much thought to how to evaluate. I had planned to use the individual reports, the group presentation grades, and the quiz grades to assess the effectiveness of the lessons.

Instead, I now decided to develop a new quiz that incorporated the students' suggested questions (see Figure 5.2). The students were asked to select one of the three possible questions, to complete some calculations, and to demonstrate their knowledge of density. Although the second set of quizzes was much more time consuming to grade, the results were remarkably better than the first. The grades were higher and the tests indicated that the students were able to calculate density and had a concrete understanding of a relatively abstract concept.

Why did the students do better on the second test? I speculated that the scores were higher because the students were able to express their understanding of the concept in methods most comfortable to them. To test my hypothesis, I asked the students to share their thoughts about the quiz in their daily journal entries. Megan wrote, "I really felt like you wanted to know my ideas instead of asking me to repeat what was taught." Juan commented, "It was really cool to be able to use what I'm good at (writing) to do a science test." Greg felt that "the quiz was okay but I prefer the first quiz 'cause it was easier for me."

Why were the students able to perform the math calculations on the second test? I had never gone over the first test or showed them how to do the density calculations. Was it because they had seen them on the first test and felt more comfortable the second time around? Had they used their textbook as a reference to learn how to set up the problems? Was it a combination of things? I decided to include the second quiz grade with the other grades. I realized that I needed to

carefully plan how I would evaluate groupwork lessons in the future.

A few days later, I was explaining what had happened to another teacher, who expressed shock that I had allowed the students to take an alternative test. I said, "I know it takes a lot more time and creativity, but I think that the students really appreciated being a part of the decision making process and having a say in how they would be evaluated. I have really seen a change in their attitude about the class. They seem more confident and they appear to be making a greater effort in the coursework." The other teacher looked at me and said, "You are doing a real disservice to your students. They need to be able to take standardized tests. If they want to go to college they have to be able to function in a traditional mode. No one is going to let them create a story or write a song. Think about their future!" Before I even had a chance to respond, the other teacher walked out.

I wanted to scream, but there was no one to hear me. My first reaction was to discredit my colleague. Who was this teacher, anyway? She didn't use groupwork as a part of her teaching, so how would she know about alternative evaluation?

But after I calmed down, her words began to penetrate. Although we had totally different philosophies about teaching and learning, I couldn't help but think about our conversation. Was I doing the students a disservice? Would alternative evaluation methods somehow hamper my students' ability to be successful on standardized exams? Is it important to match evaluation methods with teaching strategies?

CHAPTER 2

Facilitating Groupwork Interactions

In Chapter 1, the cases described many of the instructional challenges associated with collaborative groupwork. Divided into three parts—Individuals and Groups, Low-Status Students, and Interactions With Parents and Colleagues—this chapter begins with a different starting point: the personal element that makes effective groupwork happen in the classroom. The first set of cases addresses issues that range from crafting groups that support student learning to dealing with dysfunctional groups and uncooperative group members. The second set, often poignantly honest, focuses on the difficulties associated with providing low-status students equal opportunities for learning and academic success. While some teachers celebrate "breakthroughs," others share frustration around the complexity of the task. The last two cases broach problems that occur outside of the classroom: communicating with nonsupportive parents and participating in poorly planned professional development seminars. All of the narratives juxtapose the rewards of groupwork experienced by some students (and teachers) with the dilemmas posed by others who encountered difficulties with the same tasks.

A. INDIVIDUALS AND GROUPS

Case 6

Struggles With the Dynamics of Grouping

Sam and his family immigrated to the United States from Hong Kong when he was five. His first grade teacher's recollections of Sam's year in her class painted a grim picture of the difficulties he faced: he spoke limited English, his scores on the district language assessment measures indicated that his comprehension of spoken English was restricted, he was a nonreader, he struggled with most classroom activities, he cried often, and he suffered almost daily playground injuries.

I met Sam last year when he was seven and a member of my second grade class. Knowing the difficulty he'd experienced in first grade, I was eager to give him an opportunity to succeed. I was hopeful that my class, with its focus on groupwork, would work its "cooperative magic" and that his team would give him the support he needed to be successful.

As I think back on Sam's experience working with several different groups in my classroom, I realize that his story epitomizes what I consider one of the most provocative questions about groupwork—how to organize teams. It's often taken for granted that teachers intuitively know how to group children. Yet in reality, many of us struggle with the complex dynamics of grouping. When Sam entered my classroom, I assumed that groupwork would be a valuable tool for both helping him learn English and becoming successful in his academic and social endeavors. As the year progressed, however, I found that some of my expectations were realistic, while others could be called into question.

After being a teacher/advocate of hearing impaired children for 14 years, I decided to return to the regular classroom last year and accepted a second grade position. As I contemplated my new position, I became preoccupied with the concept of grouping. I had

learned to appreciate the value of groupwork while working with the 14 students in my special education classroom. It had enabled me to work with individual students while others were productively occupied. It also facilitated language acquisition by encouraging frequent and active dialogue among group members. In traditional classrooms, it appears that active communication occurs infrequently and only between the teacher and one student at a time. By contrast, groupwork allows students to have sustained dialogues with one another throughout the course of a group project.

I was also influenced by colleagues who were participating in the Brown/Campione "Fostering a Community of Learners" (FCL) project.* They reported that working together to complete a group task seemed to engender cooperation among group members and allowed each one to contribute and be appreciated for his or her particular skills and strengths. As I returned to the regular classroom, I was eager for me and my students to participate in the FCL project as well.

When the year began, I had high expectations for groupwork—it would be an effective management tool, promote student self-esteem, and encourage collaboration. Most of all, I saw it as a vital tool to facilitate dialogue among peers, which in turn would help all students— especially second language learners like Sam—increase their verbal, written, expressive, and receptive language skills. With that in mind, my task was to effectively group 29 second graders. My second grade class consisted of 12 girls and 17 boys: 74% African American, 13% Caucasian, and 13% Asian. While a few children were from middle-class families, most were from low-income or welfare families.

---

* The "Fostering a Community of Learners" project is an instructional program designed to promote both deep disciplinary understanding and the critical forms of higher literacy—reading, writing, and argumentation. It is rooted in small group structures such as research groups, jigsaw, and exhibitions.

The big question was *how* to group them. I wanted groups that were heterogeneous, nonthreatening, noncompetitive, equitable, stimulating, motivating, and most of all, cooperative. I needed to take into special account the children who were described as "at risk"—children who either were learning English as a second language or had been identified as nonreaders.

I realized that just creating groups didn't guarantee cooperative behavior, so we began talking about what it meant to work together and ways to talk to one another to ensure equal participation, asking each other, "What are you good at? What do you like to do?" We also discussed ways of choosing a group leader and how the leader would rotate to ensure that each would have a turn. We discussed the process of working together every day, soliciting suggestions and new ideas. I hoped that the process would be ongoing throughout the year.

I decided the students would work in groups of four (with the last group having five). The original groups would remain intact for four weeks, after which we would form new ones every four to six weeks. In this fashion, by the end of the year, each child would have worked with every other child in the class at least once, thus discovering that everyone has something unique to contribute.

To prepare for my task, I did some research about various theories of grouping, talked with other teachers who used groupwork, and interviewed the first grade teacher about those of my students she had taught. I decided to let the children choose their own partners for the first round of grouping. By observing the academic and social interactions within each initial group, I intended to acquaint myself with the specific needs of the children, thereby becoming prepared to fashion subsequent groups myself.

As I watched the first groups form, I noticed that Sam chose to be in a group with three other Asian boys.

Normally I would not have allowed a group that was so homogeneous, but I felt that because the other boys spoke Sam's language and were more advanced than he in English, they could assist him in acquiring English proficiency. I hoped Sam would receive the initial help and support from his team that he so desperately needed. I was eager for Sam to be recognized for any strengths that he might exhibit and to feel successful about himself. Though I had the skills as a special educator to help Sam, I realized that I was relying heavily on his group.

It was soon apparent that the group had no "magic." Instead of being mutually supportive, the boys belittled one another. The common refrain was, "You don't know how to do *any*thing." Instead of building on each other's strengths, there was only the tearing down of one another's self-image. Instead of cooperation, there was alienation.

These problems became apparent during their first cooperative task, which was to create a new invention. I told the class that each group could create any invention as long as it was useful. They had to write a description of what it looked like and how it would be used and draw a picture of it. The first step was for each group to decide what to invent. As Sam's group discussed the possibilities, Sam suggested that it would be interesting to have an umbrella that opened on command. Initially the other members seemed interested in the idea, but later they changed the command umbrella to a flying umbrella. Sam's suggestion fell by the wayside and he was left having little or no involvement in the group's decision.

After observing this, I wondered if I should intervene. Since one of the purposes of teamwork is to empower children to resolve their conflicts and make their own decisions, I hesitated. But I noticed that Sam was distressed and apparently unable to communicate his feelings, so I asked, "Did everyone have an opportunity to share their ideas?" They all nodded, but didn't say anything. Then I asked, "Is everyone satisfied with what your invention is going to do and what it's going to look like?" They nodded, but didn't say anything. I didn't pursue the situation; I was concerned that I would violate their trust and process.

Later, when I asked Sam about it, he said, "They changed everything I said…. At first they say, 'Yeah, yeah,' then they change and say, 'No, no.' They no like me."

After this conversation, I decided I needed to pay extra attention to the group's interaction. I began noticing that most often when Sam tried to explain something, the others would have a difficult time understanding him. Over and over again Sam would repeat, "No, no, I mean… ," but the others invariably lost patience and simply left him out of the conversation. It appeared that Sam's inability to be understood lowered his status in the group. Over time, a "pecking order" emerged and Sam was at the bottom.

I suspected that he would not express his frustration or feeling of inferiority for fear of retaliation from members in his group. Initially, I tried to change the pecking order by making a conscious effort to praise each of them in the same way so as to bring equitable attention to all of them, while simultaneously hoping to call attention to Sam's contribution. But no amount of positive reinforcement seemed to make a difference. It was apparent that I needed to find a common bond other than their ethnicity to help the boys redirect their competitiveness.

I didn't have to look too far. Evidence of their artistic talents was readily apparent within a few weeks as they undertook projects such as research, story writing and illustrating, mapmaking, and cooperative problem solving. As I observed them I soon learned that each had a knack for a particular skill, and they would "trade" them. One boy had an eye for color, another was skillful with proportion, the third was good with

details, and Sam was able to lay out the whole picture. The boys worked well together, "trading" their skills on projects that called for such talents. In this context, Sam's artwork became his method of communication, the "pecking order" disappeared, and Sam smiled often and laughed a lot.

The question became how to help the boys expand this "once in a while" cooperative mode into a more consistent behavior. Once again I consulted my colleagues, only to be told to disband the group and start over again. But I didn't want the group to think that they had failed. Nor did I want them to think that if something wasn't going well someone would automatically rescue them. I wrestled with my mixed feelings for a short time and decided to give the boys a choice: they could continue together for the remaining time or they could separate and work individually.

They chose to stay together. Three of the boys seemed to thrive on their relationship within the group, but Sam continued to be an odd man out who just kept trying in every way that he could to fit in with the group.

After four weeks, it was time to change groups. Because I suspected that the students would continue to group themselves by the same gender, I told the class that the new teams would consist of both boys and girls. I asked them to write on a card the names of two boys and two girls they wanted to work with. I said I would create the groups with these preferences in mind, promising that they would be in a group with at least one of their choices. Sam chose to be in a group with two very outspoken girls and a boy who was preoccupied with being entertaining. None of these children spoke Cantonese.

Unlike the other groups, this foursome quickly managed to divide itself into two pairs—the two girls in one pair and the two boys in the other. The two subgroups cooperated by subcontracting with each other just like a builder; they assigned roles to each other. Sam did all the group's artwork, the second boy was in charge of cleanup, and the girls handled all the academic work. Everyone seemed comfortable with the assigned roles. There was plenty of constructive dialogue, conflict was minimal, and projects were completed cooperatively, though not collaboratively.

This group proved especially supportive of Sam. In his previous team, Sam's fellow students made little effort either to understand what he tried to say or to elicit his contributions. By contrast, this group was more willing to listen as Sam laboriously tried to explain his thinking. I attributed this in part to their personalities, and in part to the fact that as a class we'd just spent four weeks practicing our listening skills. Also, as the tasks became increasingly complex, groups stood more to gain from engaging the skills and talents of all members.

One day when the children were working on a complicated math story about Saint Ives, Sam tried to explain his very intricate drawing and solution. As he carefully discussed each detail, the other members would stop him to seek clarification, at which point he would say, "No, no, I mean…." As he began his explanation again, the others would just look and wait patiently for him to continue. And with each opportunity to talk, Sam gained confidence in his ability to communicate.

When we regrouped again, I noticed that although Sam's receptive skills (i.e., auditory, written, and visual comprehension) remained limited, his expressive verbal skills had increased noticeably. He was talking more intelligibly and using appropriate vocabulary. His classmates reported that he was starting to talk a lot on the playground during recess. It was happening. Sam was beginning to express himself in English.

Throughout the year, Sam continued to make great progress in his verbal expressive skills. But his reading and writing skills unfortunately remained extremely limited. Some of my colleagues felt that cooperative grouping allowed Sam to become overly dependent on the members of his group. They felt that because each member contributes to a group project according to his skills, Sam wasn't forced to develop the reading and writing skills he would have needed had he been working independently. But I felt that Sam clearly benefited from the opportunities to interact with appropriate linguistic role models. I also felt strongly that as Sam continued to increase his verbal skills, his reading and writing would follow accordingly.

By the end of the year, however, Sam's behavior changed in a way I had not anticipated. His language skills increased to such an extent that he tried to assume leadership in his group, and for a while, his nonstop talking enabled him to exude confidence. Then things changed again. He began to order people around, and it appeared as if he had lost all interest in working cooperatively. Two members responded by ignoring him and the third argued with him. My own attempts to intervene—to serve as a mediator and thereby model a possible solution—met with resentment from the whole group.

Now, as I look back on last year, I realize that there is no "cooperative magic"; rather, creating groups that are cooperative and collaborative is a complex, multifaceted endeavor. Sam's involvement in group activities certainly had its ups and downs. On one hand, I am pleased with Sam's growth. When he began the year, he was in a group where he felt rejected and insecure and that his contributions had little value. In the second group, he found teammates who recognized his skills and were willing to listen and attend to his needs. Sam's confidence grew, and with it, his ability to communicate soared. His progress improved his status in subsequent groups. But by the end of the year, Sam became domineering and overbearing and tried to usurp control.

I wonder if the group process created a monster or if Sam's attempt to wield power might have been a natural step in the process of learning how to cooperate within a group setting. How much might his desire to dominate his classmates be related to his new and improved communication skills? Had he been so intent on acquiring language that he hadn't tuned into the other important factors that I consider crucial—equity and collaboration in groupwork?

I also wonder what the teacher's role is when one member of a group tries to gain control. Is it possible that what I interpret to be uncooperative behavior isn't necessarily interpreted the same way by other group members? Could this account for why Sam's last group appeared to resent my attempt to intervene in their group process?

Some groups work and some don't; why I even bother to "craft" the perfect group still mystifies me.

This case is about the year's first big group assignment, and more particularly, about a group I assembled around Daryl, one of the most interesting students I've ever taught. When I crafted the groups, I worked hard to get it just right so each group was well qualified to cooperate, write, and generate a creative response to a difficult assignment. As each group completed the five-day poetry assignment, I wanted increased learning, cooperation, tolerance, and a diversity of skills and attitudes. What I saw in Daryl's group still puzzles me.

I am a sixth-year English teacher frustrated by my department's tracking of students. Currently I teach at least one section of each track: general, college preparatory, and honors. This situation took place in my sophomore honors English class, where most of the students were "good" at school, came from "good" homes, and had parents who'd graduated from college. What happens when you get a kid who doesn't come from a "good" home and whose parents haven't graduated from college?

Daryl transferred to our school from the "weak" working-class high school in the district. He arrived on the third day of school with a recommendation and an "A" from his freshman college prep teacher; he also came speaking slang, writing run-ons, and willing to be brutally honest in his oral and written work.

Even though Daryl hadn't prepared for this class by reading the four required summer reading books, I took him in. In his written application for the class, he indicated a willingness to do whatever work was necessary. He also said he liked reading and needed work on his writing. I wondered if he would feel alienated among a group of students who come from middle- and upper-middle-class families.

In many ways, Daryl stuck out. He wore a cap as he slyly munched on sandwiches and sipped Cokes in the back of the class, where I've never allowed eating for fear of rodents. He said "pissed off" when asked how a particular character acted. His classmates didn't know how to react. Should they look at me? At Daryl? Or share a snickering glance with a friend? *They* didn't speak slang in class. Daryl also managed to read within the first week two books from the required summer reading list, *1984* and *Cry, the Beloved Country*.

One of his first essays stunned me. Daryl argued that Petruchio from *The Taming of the Shrew* was right about his outlook on women. He compared his labor-intensive summer work to his sister's. "I feel white collars are wienne [sic] jobs and wives can bitch all they want (or husbands). Second, the work load of my sister was minimal. If you were to take a household of four or more kids I can see sympathy for wives (or husbands) who take care of them. Nuff said!"

When I have a student who sticks out—for whatever reason—it is always difficult deciding which group to put him in. Something tells me that if I formed groups at random, they would work as constructively as the groups I so carefully compose. Assembling a group around Daryl took some careful thought. I feared that with the wrong students, Daryl would have a horrible experience in this "goodie-goodie" honors class. Conversely, I hoped that with the right students, Daryl would catch some of their enthusiasm for school. At the same time, I thought that any one of my students could benefit from working with Daryl, if not so much for the raw way he tackled things as for the experience of working with someone different from the kids they had always worked with on this perpetual honors track.

With Daryl I placed Kara, one of my best students whose stellar beginning-of-the-year writing seemed to bode well for good groupwork. I searched the roll book for nice kids, whom I figured would be tolerant. I nabbed Josh, who seemed especially mature and nice. I liked how he had complimented my independent reading list and asked for more recommendations. I also added Elizabeth, a quirky young woman who had sworn off pants and who probably would have been just as happy wearing her long skirts at the turn of the century.

This group worked together off and on for five to six weeks, primarily in writing response groups. I had hoped that by the time we reached the culminating project for the poetry unit, the groups would be well oiled and ready to work on a more extended task.

For this unit, the students studied poetry terminology, practiced different ways of reading and reacting to poems, wrote short poems, and learned how to write about poetry. The unit culminated with a five-day group project, for which, in retrospect, I probably had set up too many objectives.

I wanted the students to synthesize what they had learned about poetry, writing about poetry, and appreciating poetry… *and* I wanted them to teach their classmates. The assignment had many tasks, each drawing upon their abilities to apply what they had learned in the previous weeks of poetry and writing instruction.

First, each group had to reread a quarter of our class poetry anthology (10 or so pages), comprising poems the students had brought from home. Each group member then nominated one poem that would be good for the group to write about, "unpack," and "present" to class. The group then spent a day discussing the choices and reaching consensus. In their presentations to the class, I wanted the group members to get their classmates to understand and appreciate the poem. I asked that in addition to doing a presentation, the groups submit a "poetry packet," to include paragraphs of analysis that the students wrote individually (with the help of peer response), an artistic rendering of the poem, and notes explaining the process by which the group had planned their group poetry presentation.

For the first day, I randomly selected facilitators, timers, and note-takers, reminding students to rotate these jobs each day. I pointed out that other jobs would come up that were more specifically related to the tasks: idea editors, copy editors, artists, and presenters.

On the day Daryl, Kara, Elizabeth, and Josh tried to reach a consensus about which poem to pursue, I watched, growing increasingly disappointed.

Were they trying to reach a consensus? Did they know how? Daryl and Elizabeth sat facing Kara and Josh. Sagging in his chair, Daryl gazed away, pointing his outstretched legs toward another group. Elizabeth, disgusted, looked down as she paged through the anthology. Across from them Josh and Kara talked animatedly.

When I stopped at their group, Kara told me the group had chosen Raymond Carver's poem "Gravy." Elizabeth complained that no one was listening to her and that she hated "the dumb poem they both want." I immediately worried that the "both" Elizabeth referred to meant that Kara and Josh were the decision makers.

I've always got a million questions about teaching. Now I wondered if I should get involved or let them work it out. In this situation, I decided to step in. Kara and Josh volunteered that "Gravy" would work well. Apparently none of the other three wanted to work with the short but confusing Emily Dickinson poem Elizabeth had selected. And Daryl proclaimed, "I *really* don't care which poem *they* want." Without offering advice, I moved on. They ended up selecting "Gravy."

The next couple of days, I observed the group diligently working on the written assignment. Daryl repeatedly came to me with his own paragraph, only to be sent back to the group. I could just see him yawning as he handed his writing over to Elizabeth or Kara: "Go on, you look at it… *he* won't."

Daryl would often search me out to say, "We're done. Now what should we do?"

"Ask your group," I'd say.

"They told me to ask you."

"Tell them that as a group you need to figure out and practice your presentation." Such noncommunicative conferences took place while other groups gained momentum and enthusiasm as they finished their written work and planned their presentations.

Finally the day came for their presentation of "Gravy." I hated watching it. Kara and Josh read alternating stanzas of the poem in a self-important way, while Elizabeth, wearing a checkered apron over her long skirt, mixed up some real gravy. Daryl stood aside with nothing to do. Then, in an unrehearsed moment that distracted from the presentation, he reached for the gravy, taking a few licks. Other than that, the initial selectors of the poem, Kara and Josh, had taken over the presentation. The other two never really found their way into the project.

In my response to the presentation, I wrote separate comments for each individual and for the group: "Kara and Josh dominate too much. I'd like to hear Elizabeth and Daryl speak more." I reminded Daryl to "avoid eating during presentation; you take away attention from others." I warned Kara to be "careful of giggling—maintain composure." I made no positive comments. By contrast, I included positive comments on every other group's grade sheet.

I was so disappointed in this group that I couldn't be positive. In the preceding days I could have coached them into being more collaborative. But not knowing how, I had just glared at them.

After the project, I asked each student to respond independently to three questions:

1. What jobs did you take on during the course of this project?
2. How would you rate your own use of time for this project?
3. Finish the following statements and support them: I think, as a member of my group, I helped by ___, and I (dis)liked how my group ___.

Daryl reported that his time had been "wasted because everyone says the same thing over and hasn't concentrated on the presentation [which] is the true group 'thang.' " Daryl also said he disliked how his group worked "because everyone discussed their own personal problems and many times me and Josh were out of the picture."

Elizabeth noted that she had taken "rather skimpy notes for the group" and had done "many drafts of [her] paragraph, highlighting, typing, and defining." She'd "drawn the picture, redone it, and stressed out." She said she resented the fact the two boys in the group hadn't done their share.

Josh, as it turned out, had had an unsettling retreat experience during the weekend prior to this poetry project. He confessed that he had used class time to work out personal problems rather than to work on the assignment. "I think my use of class time has been not so great because I have not been really with it for the past several days," he wrote. "I know that if I had been in a little better mental state, I would have devoted more time and energy into these class time activities." The irony is that I had put Josh in the group precisely because of his good energy in class.

Kara, the group's academic achiever, who took control so she wouldn't lose control, said, "I liked how *most* of my group worked because we got our goals accomplished and we actively helped each other. Unfortunately, Daryl didn't seem interested in working, which hurt our progress, although we tried to include him."

Each of the students recognized that they hadn't been completely successful. Elizabeth blamed the young men in the group; Kara blamed Daryl; Daryl blamed the group; Josh blamed himself.

Despite the less-than-successful group process and presentation, the quality of the individually written paragraphs far surpassed every other group's. Each student clearly understood various points about "Gravy." The paragraphs were notable for their clarity, use of appropriate evidence, and commentary. They were largely free of mechanical errors, too. To me, their high-quality written work indicated that the group had successfully given meaningful response for revisions.

I'm not sure how I could have altered the group's experience. Maybe my precepts for group construction were wrong. I had always thought that a teacher should place one highly motivated anchor in each group. In this case though, I made the assumption—wrongly—that an academic star is also talented at interpersonal group skills. I've always tried to create groups that have both genders represented. Perhaps in this case, Daryl might have benefited more from an all-boy group.

I had wanted the group presentations to have some magical component, and most did. But it was an optimistic leap on my part to think that just because other students had succeeded in groups, some magic would occur every time in every group.

I still wonder how this group could fail so miserably in one aspect of the assignment, yet apparently succeed on another. Maybe its success on the written task could be attributed to the five weeks of paragraph writing and revision we had completed before this project. Or maybe the group *did* know how to respond and revise, but those skills don't necessarily transfer to the type of consensus building necessary to prepare the poetry presentation.

As for Daryl—just as suddenly as he had ridden into my class on the third day of school, he rode out again during the winter holiday, heading for Nebraska with his Dad. Damn it, I wasn't ready for him to just pick up and go.

Case 8

My Struggle With Sharon

Boldly striding through the narrow doorway, her wild, mouse brown curls trailing, Sharon straddles her desk, bellowing her arrival. With her Raiders jacket draped down to her knees, she loudly cracks her gum, signaling that class can now begin—Sharon Dims is ready, pen in hand and mouth agape.

Groupwork with Sharon is not easy—for her or for the others in her group. She is the type of student who wants to work only with her "best" friend, whether the two are in the same class or not. Because of this Sharon often cuts class, wandering around the school searching for Angie, or she arrives late because she and Angie *"had* to talk." This usually means she has missed the directions and is unsure of the assignment. So her group, now responsible for telling Sharon what the assignment is, has less time to work on the tasks.

I teach eighth grade Language Arts core in a Northern California middle school. Our student population is approximately 60% Hispanic, 25% Caucasian, and 10% African American. The remaining 5% includes Pacific Islander, Asian, and Middle Eastern students. Except for the GATE class and Sheltered English instruction classes, our students are grouped heterogeneously. In my morning class, which is Sharon's, I have 24 students, half of whom are Resource Special Education Pupils (RSP). Due to the large number of students who are either RSP or Limited English Proficient (LEP), I tend to choose group assignments carefully so all students will feel fairly successful.

This year my classroom theme was friendship and responsibility, and I decided I would like the students to learn these concepts through "doing." Come December and the holiday season, I developed an assignment in which students worked cooperatively to create Christmas presents for children in a local hospital. The assignment, which was to be done in groups of four, was to write and illustrate an original children's story that contained a moral, a main character (either an animal or a person), and an adventure to illustrate the moral. Students were to illustrate the story using only four colors—not counting black or white. The model for our stories were Gerald McDermott's books: *Anansi the Spider, Zomo the Rabbit, Arrow to the Sun, Papagayo the Parrot,* and *The Stone Cutter.* The groups were given three days of class time to work on their original stories. I also encouraged the students to exchange telephone numbers so they could work outside of class. At the end of the three days, the stories were to be presented to the class and then given to the children in the hospital. In the past, it seemed easier for students to write individually, seeking peer response to their drafts from one other student. It occurred to me that having four students create one story with illustrations might be difficult to manage, especially with this class. My past experience with their group dynamics told me these students were hard to manage because of their short attention spans and their difficulty getting and staying on task.

The students in this class had worked in groups on numerous projects, but never on one that was so encompassing. I decided we would begin work on a Thursday, and on the preceding Monday I carefully placed the students in groups according to ability (e.g., artistic, writing), skills (e.g., literary, comprehension), and personality (e.g., bossy, congenial). I wanted to give them four days to adjust to each other. Because this task required both artistic and literary abilities and skills, I tried to place in each group at least one student who had shown artistic interest, as well as one student who enjoyed writing and being creative.

When Thursday arrived, 12 students were out of the class on a trip. Instead of postponing the assignment, I decided to try it anyway. I carefully recrafted groups from the remaining students. I tried to include in each group a high achiever, a low achiever, an average student, and a nonachiever.

Group 3 was composed of Sharon, Roy, Alicia, and Charles. Alicia, a high achiever, always tries her hardest to please her parents, peers, and teachers, both academically and socially. She is always the leader in a group, making sure the task is done on time and completed in a beautiful, well-planned manner. Charles is the low achiever. He is undersized for his age, sickly, and generally immature. But he is quite agreeable and works well in a group. He will follow directions and does make an effort. Roy is average. He works to complete the task and will follow the lead of those he works with. He always tries, and he usually has his work in on time.

Sharon is the nonachiever. She rarely starts assignments, let alone completes them. In addition to not doing the work, she whines and complains: "I don't understand the directions." "What do you want *me* to do?" "Tell *me* again." Sharon also tends to be bossy and does not understand directions from peers very well. I hoped by placing her in a group with three quiet people who worked well she would get on task and join the others. I also assigned roles: Alicia, the facilitator; Sharon, the reporter; Roy, the recorder; and Charles, the gatherer/harmonizer. I thought Alicia would get the group going, and I knew Sharon would be pleased to be the reporter. She liked to be the center of attention, and being the reporter would guarantee that.

I gave the class directions and told the recorder to write down the instructions from the board and record all the ideas and general information about their groups as they were working. I also reminded the facilitators that their job was to facilitate, not to boss.

The students seemed to get down to business right away. Walking around the room, I stopped to ask each group what they had decided about their story's moral and characters. Glancing at group 3, I saw trouble brewing and walked over to see what was going on. Sharon started shouting that Alicia wanted the group to do her story idea and not Sharon's. She insisted that Alicia was being bossy and said she wouldn't work on

Alicia's project. "Why is Alicia always the leader?" she asked.

I tried valiantly to stick to my role by speaking only to the facilitator,* in this case, Alicia. When I inquired how the group was progressing, Alicia, in a soft, strong voice, told me that she had only been sticking to her role as facilitator and had been explaining the task. She was merely making suggestions about theme and the boys had liked them, she said. Only Sharon hadn't. As Alicia was explaining this to me, Sharon kept interrupting to call her a liar.

Desperately wanting this group to get on task, I told Alicia to try harder. I suggested that maybe Sharon's ideas were terrific and could be a real asset to the story. In fact, I suggested, perhaps the group could compromise and weave each other's ideas into one story.

As I left the group, I hoped they would work out their differences and produce a finished story they would all be proud of. I was pleased that Sharon at least was interested in the project, and I hoped that Alicia, in her desire to achieve, would allow Sharon to become a positive force, not a negative one as she had been in the past. As I walked away, the group was talking loudly, but it was about the project, so I decided not to interfere further.

I tried not to stare at group 3. I heard their voices— Sharon's, in particular, louder than the others'—but they were on task. I circulated among the groups, making sure all the students were working. Later, arriving back at group 3, I was greeted by a whine from Sharon, who said she was absolutely, positively not working with this group, that I should just write her a

---

* According to the workshop on groupwork, the roles are carefully detailed, and the teacher is to speak only to the facilitator. The students are to try to solve their problems in the group. If they decide they need specific information from the teacher, it is the role of the facilitator to ask. The teacher's role is that of an outsider, to assist or guide only when necessary.

referral for disobedience and defiance. I told Sharon she was not getting out of the work, that the group had to persevere. I reminded all four that theirs was a group project and all would get the same grade.** I also reminded them that part of the grade was based on their cooperation. I then walked away, not wanting to hear any comments from Sharon.

A short time later, Alicia quietly and unobtrusively came up to me and said, "I'm sorry, Mrs. Forest, it's not working. I am trying my hardest, but Sharon will not cooperate. Please, can you move me to another group?" I fully understood what Alicia meant, because I too had experienced Sharon's orneriness. I moved Alicia into another group.

The day of presentations arrived. Alicia and her new group had created a wonderful story and presented it perfectly. The story contained all required elements, and the illustrations were beautifully drawn. The group members talked about how they had settled their differences by using *Roshambu*, a children's game for making decisions. Alicia later told me it was easier to work with a group that wanted the story to look and sound good, and that she liked working with a group that found positive, fun solutions to problems.

When group 3 presented, their story was the one that Alicia had suggested in the beginning. As Sharon explained, "It was a good story, but it was Alicia's when she was in the group. With her gone, it became ours!" Group 3's story contained all the required elements, but the pictures were sloppily drawn, the writing contained many spelling and grammar errors, and its overall appearance was one that showed minimal care and effort. Even so, I applauded their endeavor in completing the project and presenting their story to the class.

I'm not sure what Sharon or Alicia learned from this experience, but I am sure what it taught me about groupwork and human nature. All students, even nonachievers like Sharon, want to be successful. It was interesting that group 3 stayed with the ideas originally presented by Alicia. Perhaps I should have encouraged Sharon instead of Alicia, or maybe I shouldn't have put them together in the beginning. In the future, I will probably not put Sharon with a strong personality like Alicia, and hope that she learns to cooperate with all students, not just the ones who follow her.

For me, several questions arose from this experience. Was I wrong in encouraging Alicia to cooperate, instead of focusing on Sharon and encouraging her to be more cooperative? Should I form groups by lottery and not try to make all groups equal in abilities and skills? How can I distinguish successful student growth in this particular project if I allow students to move to other groups when they encounter problems? Should I have allowed failure?

**We were taught that the goal is that all students work together and that each possesses a skill that can contribute to the final project. Some skills are not necessarily academic, some are in interaction and facilitating students working together.

Case 9

To Be, or "Not"

I am a twenty-something male in my fourth year of teaching. I teach earth and physical science to eighth graders at a middle school located in a middle-class neighborhood of a large California city. My students are mostly from the neighborhood, with a large number of bus riders from other areas of the city.

I strongly believe working in groups is good for the socialization process. The adage that "we teach kids, not subjects" often holds true for me as a middle school teacher. Social skills, problem solving and decision making, personal crisis management, and acceptable behavior are often topics of discussion in my classroom. Like most science classes these days, my class is geared toward hands-on labwork, toward "doing" science rather than reading about science—which is as it should be. I believe that doing an experiment for yourself multiplies the amount and degree of learning that occurs. So while running labs for my students is much more time and energy consuming for me, I enjoy it, and my students overwhelmingly agree that labs are preferable to any other classroom activity. Additionally, the hands-on work gives kids who normally don't like school something to enjoy.

Optimally, most labwork is performed in pairs, but that's made impossible by the realities of a shrinking budget, limited supplies, and a room providing only six lab stations for 30 or more students. My students usually work on lab and other activities in groups of four. To prevent cliques from forming and to manage any behavior problems that develop, I change group membership often (whenever I get around to it).

I am often forced to adapt lab projects designed for two students to accommodate the necessity of groups of four. I have found most lab activities easily adaptable to fours, as long as there is enough work so everyone has something to do. However, because of a ridiculous classroom architecture in which the sinks and Bunsen burner outlets are directly against the wall and beneath low-hanging cabinets with fluorescent light fixtures

attached, physical and visual access to experiments can be a problem for groups larger than two.

Students are responsible for participating appropriately in their groups: following lab rules, not disrupting other groups, and cleaning up. They are also responsible for turning in individual work, so they cannot rely totally on their partners.

When conflicts arise within the group, I try to allow the students to work them out before I intervene. Occasionally I remove disruptive students or those who do not follow lab safety standards. In addition, if an entire group becomes dysfunctional, I may shut it down for part of a period.

I assign groups randomly, more or less, so by the end of the year each student has had the opportunity to work with his or her friends several times, as well as the misfortune to work with the dreaded *nots* ("Not him!" "Not her!") on one or more occasions. This allows students to learn by experience that they can work with anyone, even though it may take some effort. It is also an attempt at simulating life outside the classroom, because as we all know, in the real world you always get stuck with a "not." So I rarely listen to the cries and pleas ("But we don't get along!"), telling students that if they get stuck with a "not" this time, next time someone else will probably feel the same way about being stuck with *them*, so it all evens out in the end.

In one class, I found very few "nots," if any. The kids all seemed to accept each other and were willing to work with whomever I assigned them. Very early in the year, however, I found the exceptions in this seemingly idyllic setting: Dennis and Caroline. In no uncertain terms, each individually told me about his or her dislike for the other. In the unique language of eighth graders, they hated each other's guts. Their hatred was so intense that when either of them made a comment or asked or answered a question, the other would make a face, roll his or her eyes, or mumble something less than polite in an all-too-audible sotto voce. In short, they behaved like siblings. Were these the rumblings of a love–hate relationship, a case of simply not knowing each other well enough, or perhaps the result of an unresolved elementary school conflict?

Whatever the cause of their dislike, I intentionally kept them separated to avoid any unnecessary conflict during groupwork, as well as in their regular seating. That changed the week before winter vacation, when I was too tired to realize what I was doing and too preoccupied to care. On that fateful day, toward the end of a chemistry unit, when the luck of the draw brought Dennis and Caroline together to work on a two-day lab, their other partners, Scott, Patrick, and Lydia, must have thought *they* were being punished for something.

Dennis and Caroline both checked the group assignment chart as they came in, dutiful students that they are, and immediately came over to protest. I considered switching them to avoid the war they both assured me would soon follow. Although they finally convinced me of the grievous error I had committed, I decided to leave the assignment and just monitor their group carefully. I didn't want to set a precedent that went against my beliefs and goals for groupwork, one which would surely come back to haunt me: "But you let Dennis and Caroline switch!"

For this particular lab, my two objectives were for students to become more familiar with real-life chemistry, in terms of using equipment and carrying out a test that chemists actually use, and for them to improve their thinking and problem solving skills. The lab involved a simple procedure by which groups could distinguish a number of chemicals by their reaction with a gas flame. I emphasized in my opening statements that students were to carefully observe the color of the flame, possibly making several tests with each compound, and describe the color as accurately as possible. The last part of the lab involved a problem solving activity in which the students were to identify some unknown compounds by comparing them to known compounds. The actual amount of work to be done was minimal, but this lab had never failed to captivate my students.

No sooner had the groups begun working than Caroline and Dennis began raising their voices at each other: "No, you're doing that wrong…" "No, we already used that one…" "Let me do it, you're doing it wrong…" "That's the wrong color…" "You're hogging it…" They were loud, but I let them work on with only a stern glance to show I was keeping an eye on them. After a few minutes of fairly quiet work, they began getting angry, and once again voices were raised as names were called and more accusations were hurled. This time, as I watched from across the room, Caroline and Dennis began almost wrestling each other for control of the equipment.

The little "I-told-you-so" voice in my head finally spoke up. Had I goofed? Could I still remain on the sidelines? Had they gone too far? Would one of the other students take control? What was I to do?

I decided it was time to step in. I told them they were finished working and sent the entire group out of the room. I took a few minutes to compose my thoughts and threats and then met them outside. We reviewed the lab safety instructions for working with Bunsen burners, and then I asked what the problem was. Caroline and Dennis were openly hostile, each interrupting and blaming the other for the group's failure, while Lydia, Scott, and Patrick said they had no idea what had happened. Were these three being honest? Were they simply covering for the others in hopes of being allowed to go back inside? Or were they afraid of ratting on Caroline and Dennis?

I chose not to take the time to decide who was at fault. I was angry that they could not solve their problem on their own, and that the problem had come up during my class. I was not in the mood to mediate or arbitrate, and if they were not going to own up, I did not care that possibly innocent people were being punished.

Rather than spend the rest of the period refereeing, I decided to have the group attempt a social skills activity instead of a chemistry lesson. I instructed all five of them not to work on the lab, but to come up with a plan of action that would allow them to complete the rest of the lab the next day. They were not to continue the lab that day or the next if they could not ensure that they would be able to complete it without my intervention. I heard them discussing *something* in loud voices, but I did not check back with them during the period. I did allow them into the room to clean up their lab station before they left.

The next day the class resumed the lab. As promised, Dennis and Caroline's group assured me that they were ready with a foolproof plan for their group, conceived of by Caroline and agreed to by Dennis. So I let them begin working. With only a few minor flare-ups, they worked the entire period and completed the lab. I could see on Dennis's face and hear in Caroline's voice the restraint they were showing. They did an admirable job, and I wished them an enjoyable vacation as I shooed them out the door after class.

When the class returned from winter vacation, I left the same groupings for the next lab, also a two-day affair. I again monitored Caroline and Dennis's group and this time heard and saw a much more workable environment, although they certainly were not one big happy family. There was still a good deal of hostility, although it was dealt with in a much more civilized way.

I asked Caroline and Dennis to come and speak with me separately after school about their group. Caroline told me that she and Dennis "just don't get along" and never had. She felt the cause of the problem was that all of her group members wanted to get involved, yet there wasn't enough for each of them to do. She admitted that although she had blamed Dennis for causing the

fiasco, the real obstacle to completing the lab was a communication breakdown in which one person was giving information while another was testing a second chemical, another was trying to verify which materials had already been used, and no one was listening to anyone. Her solution was for everyone to pay attention to each other and take turns doing the actual testing so that everyone could have a chance to do something. She told me she thought she and Dennis had learned to work together when necessary, but that they still did not get along any better.

In retrospect, Caroline made a valid point: there wasn't enough in this lab to keep five people engaged, a situation that had caused a lot of the initial frustration. Yet it was worth it for me to let them struggle through their frustration with the lab and with each other, and I feel it was worth it for them. They both came away with the knowledge that they had successfully solved a major problem that had prevented them from doing the lab, and that both might be better prepared if a similar situation ever arose.

Dennis's comments were much the same. He described himself and Caroline as "control freaks." Each of them wanted to be in charge, and the other three group members were willing to allow that to happen. Dennis did not blame himself nor anyone else for the group's failure; in his eyes it was no one's fault. His solution was to give everyone a specific job to do, allowing each person to participate without interference from the others. If the others felt that one person's judgment was in error, each could write whatever they wanted; if they felt the person had made an inaccurate test, they were free to repeat the test later. Dennis agreed that he and Caroline could now work together again, if necessary, but said he found that he was able to work with just about anyone anyway. And no, he didn't see any improvement in their personal relationship as a result of their working together.

In my own analysis, this activity had the potential for trouble, since it was neither designed for five gung-ho students working in a crowded environment nor adaptable to it. Although this was the only negative incident I've ever encountered with this lab, one way to prevent a repeat would be to have only half the class at a time work on the lab. But this creates other problems: multiple lesson plans, inattentiveness by nonpartici-pants, and extra supervision. In addition, I see that Caroline and Dennis have personalities that clash. Since neither is willing to give in or compromise unless forced, working together is difficult for them. I still believe that any two people can work together if necessary, and since we rarely get to choose our work-ing associates as adults, the more practice we get working with the "nots" on a temporary basis, the less painful it will be when we get stuck with one of them permanently.

Later on, Caroline wrote me a note saying that a few days afterward Dennis had come to her and offered a truce. She accepted.

Case 10

Confronting One Group's Inertia

"Aw, Mrs. Weston, do we have to do this?" "What are we supposed to do anyway?" "I don't understand!"

Comments like these poured forth when I introduced the activity for collaborative groups to my freshman reading class. Still, I smiled confidently.

I'm an African American woman who has been teaching for 15 years, and I had just completed a training workshop in collaborative groupwork. There I had heard many reasons why this method of classroom instruction is exceptionally effective. Now, back in my classroom, I was convinced that once my students began to work together on the assignment, rich interactions would develop.

This prospect was particularly exciting because these students were low achievers. Their reading scores generally fell between grade levels 4.0 and 6.8. The class included most of the minorities on campus as well as some of the school's least corrigible students. Approximately 75% were bused to the school daily from a low-income community 15 miles away. Difficulty competing academically with others at their grade level had burdened many with feelings of inferiority. Some became buffoons or bullies. Few would admit to their lack of basic skills or the extent of their struggle with printed text.

The task I devised was to give each group a poem illustrating a particular poetic form along with activities to help them examine it together. My intent was not to foster expertise in poetic verse, but to help students develop cooperative learning skills. Groupwork would give each student an opportunity to help complete the task by sharing her own special talents and understanding.

First, however, the students needed some preparation. Before giving them the assignment, I introduced the idea of imagery. We explored images through the five senses, read familiar poetic pieces, and discussed how images were expressed in them. The students then wrote their own short pieces, emulating the examples. In these ways, I introduced them to each poetic term they would later encounter in their groups.

Equally important, before this lesson, I engaged the class in several activities designed to build group trust and cohesiveness. These activities, focusing on listening skills, respect for others, and being a polite audience, were suggested at the seminar on groupwork. They set the stage for open exchange by diminishing the fear of "Who's going to laugh at me?"

I selected groups arbitrarily. By chance, four boys who were enrolled in my class to improve their reading skills were grouped together. For the first few minutes after the class separated into groups, these four sat quietly, desks askew, each retreating into his own separate world. They didn't look at each other or speak. I was determined to give them an opportunity to break the ice and at least begin discussing the task before I intervened. They continued to sit nervously and wait, knowing that I would eventually rescue them.

One boy pulled his hood up and rested his head on the desk. With his face hidden, he withdrew completely from the group. Another pulled out a pencil stub and began filling a sheet of paper with drawings of .45 magnum handguns. He nonchalantly swayed his head and made sounds like guns firing. The other two boys sat awkwardly for a few minutes, then began a game of tic-tac-toe that soon grew intense and noisy. All four gave the impression they didn't care if the group worked together or not.

When they saw me glance in their direction, the tic-tac-toe players began complaining that the group just wouldn't work together. They asked to be changed to another group. The hooded student lifted his head and sullenly announced he couldn't work because I hadn't personally told him what to do. Ironically, he was the designated facilitator, responsible for ensuring that the others were interacting.

By this time I was becoming uncomfortable. I walked to the group and spoke to the hooded student. "Do you have questions about your responsibilities in the facilitator's role?" I asked. I instructed him to review the board where the list of duties for each role was described. He slid down further in his chair and said, "What are we supposed to do?" Pointing to the activity sheets, I asked if his group had read the instructions for the task. The others began to joke nervously about the facilitator's ability to read. I glared sharply, and they quickly muffled their laughter. But I was disappointed to see that there had been little transfer of the politeness skills we'd worked on in advance of the actual groupwork.

Turning back to the facilitator, I suggested that the group consider reading the task to see what understanding they could glean from the instructions. I also suggested that they turn their desks around to face each other to create a bit of group togetherness. Before any of them could again voice their confusion or helplessness, I quickly exited, promising to return shortly to check their progress.

They continued to grumble and complain about having to sit in groups to do a dumb assignment that the teacher refused to explain. Finally, one of the boys said to no one in particular, "What does that assignment sheet say, anyway?" The others didn't respond.

When I returned to the group a little later, they began blaming each other for being unable to get started. The facilitator said his group was dumb and wouldn't work. They all agreed that the assignment was just too hard. I couldn't tell whether they actually couldn't understand the instructions or were just saying so as an excuse to avoid getting started.

My first inclination was to read the assignment sheet to them while explaining exactly what they were to do. But because I wanted to encourage them to become independent learners able to rely on the special talents that each brought to the group, I felt I had to allow them time to flounder as part of the process of getting comfortable with groupwork. I was optimistic that they would ultimately start interacting and trust their own insights rather than simply wait for me to give them mine.

By the end of the period, however, the group still had not begun to work together. The facilitator remained withdrawn and uninvolved. The rest of the group took its cue from him and found distractions. Much to my chagrin, little spitballs flew across the room from their direction. I sighed, feeling my earlier enthusiasm for groupwork beginning to wane. As the class was leaving, the budding artist who had spent much of his time drawing guns frowned apologetically and said, "You know, Mrs. Weston, poetry is just not my thing!" Drawing pictures apparently was.

I tried to analyze what had gone wrong. What could have helped this group, other than totally reassigning its members or doing the assignment for them? Students often learn to be dependent upon teachers by feigning helplessness. Aware of this—and of my penchant for rescuing students—I had fought the temptation to take over. I decided now to work with the group a little more to help build their confidence. But I would take care not to encourage their dependency.

The next day I sat with them for the first few minutes and suggested ways they might get started. I said they might allow Darren—whom I had determined had low status in the group—to read the instructions orally. As Darren read, the group appeared to listen intently. But when he finished, they barraged me with questions about what they should do next and how I thought they should solve the problem. I quickly left, wanting them to discuss on their own how to proceed. At last they were interacting!

Unfortunately, their discussion soon fizzled. They returned to their previous inertia. Their problem appeared not to be the level of difficulty of the assignment but their reluctance to risk exposing themselves to failure in front of their peers. After all, each had his own reputation and macho image to uphold.

When it was time for each group to make its presentation, all four slid down in their seats and tried to appear invisible. Under protest, they finally sauntered to the front, their pants dragging on their hips. They appeared embarrassed and joked to hide their discomfort while the class impatiently waited for them to begin. The reporter for the group explained that the group had fooled around and hadn't told him what to say. Before returning to their seats, they admitted they hadn't been very serious about the assignment, and that's why they had no presentation. I was pleased with their honesty and remarked to the class that their admission displayed a level of maturity.

In the discussion that followed, the class explored the problem of how to handle uncooperative group members. Students contributed ideas on how to get group members to share. They suggested, for example, that asking everyone in the group to express ideas and then listening to all comments without criticism would help to make everyone feel like an important part of the group. The class also concluded that trust was one of the biggest factors in group success. Members must feel comfortable to share without fear of being put down or having their ideas ridiculed.

The class, then, benefited from this activity because the four boys provided them with a prime example of a dysfunctional group. But was this a positive outcome for the boys involved? What was the effect on them of having their dysfunction exposed to the class? If that effect was negative, were the merits of groupwork

undermined? In pondering these questions, I resolved that in the future I would exert more control over the one area that may have contributed to the group's demise: group mix. I would attempt to use arbitrary grouping less, instead striving to guarantee a more heterogeneous mix of students.

B. Low-Status Students

Dennis was one of the B-Boys—a name bestowed almost affectionately by the front office upon a group of thuggish, low-achieving boys who all happened to have last names that began with the letter "B." By October they would all have shirts with bulldogs silk-screened on them, a symbol that identified them with a nearby street gang.

Just a little too thin, and slightly drooped at the shoulders, Dennis was an expert at being disengaged in class and a master magician whose greatest trick was making himself invisible. His book would be open, his paper and pencil ready, but closer inspection would reveal, instead of history notes, page after page of drawings—guns, gang graffiti, and comic book heroes.

Not too long after school started, I realized that Dennis might have a tough time making it through my inner-city eighth grade class. In hopes of helping him along, I decided to apply some of the things I'd learned the previous summer in a seminar on Complex Instruction.* With Dennis, I intended to test its promise that low achievers improve academically when participating in open-ended groupwork activities, and that student learning increases in proportion to student interaction. I wondered whether Dennis would become a better student as a result of participating in groupwork.

In the beginning, I hadn't pushed Dennis. Given the contrast between his poor academic record and his average test scores, I assumed that teachers had already pushed, cajoled, embarrassed, and punished Dennis in hopes of jump-starting his interest—all with little success. I doubted that I alone could spark his curiosity,

---

* Complex Instruction, developed at Stanford University, is a groupwork model that emphasizes the development of higher-order thinking skills in heterogeneous classrooms. It addresses issues of status that arise in small groups.

but hoped that Dennis's peers might be successful where teachers had failed. I decided to let the group projects entice him.

My teacher instincts told me that as others valued Dennis's contributions, he would strive harder and improve academically. While he was not great at reading and writing, he had a natural talent for drawing—an intellectual strength that would be in high demand, since many group projects require analyzing and creating visual representations. On the other hand, part of Dennis's strategy for remaining invisible was to answer every question with the same response. Whether it was a standard "check-in-and-see-if-he's-paying-attention" question or a "high-interest/no-right-answer" question, his answer was always the same: "I don't know." Not surprisingly, his classmates perceived him as being intellectually weak.

Knowing that the low expectations of his peers would inhibit Dennis's ability to participate fully in the small group projects, I planned to alter their expectations by assigning competence to Dennis, whenever possible taking special care to point out his intellectual abilities. This is the opposite of the "pull yourself up by your bootstraps" approach teachers often use with students in groupwork. It proved harder than I had anticipated, however, because initially at least, Dennis contributed nothing to the group's work.

He would not read in front of his group, nor would he draw anything for the project. His standard response was, "I can't draw that." When students discovered that he was going to be in their group, they would shrug their shoulders and roll their eyes. They would complain to me and give Dennis bad evaluations on their feedback sheets. I tried everything I could think of to improve the situation: I spoke to Dennis, I spoke to individuals in his groups, and I carefully constructed his groups so he would be with supportive and accepting students. As often as possible, I put Dennis in a group whose project required artistic ability. Finally, thanks to my suggestions and direct interventions, the other students got the idea and began to try harder to at least nominally include Dennis, continuing to ask him to draw their ideas.

Slowly, Dennis responded. In November he drew a tricycle by way of constructing a metaphor for the three branches of government. In early February he drew some illustrations for a children's book about cowboys. But in the end, these drawings alone were not enough for Dennis to pass my classes.

Dennis earned straight Fs in English and social studies over four marking periods. Academically, he wasn't making strides. I had looked for every opportunity to assign competence to Dennis, but they were few and far between, given his lack of involvement in any activity other than drawing, which itself was sporadic. I had given him help in reading, talked to his counselor, and had conferences with Dennis, all to no avail. By April it was clear to Dennis, to me, and to the other students that he would not go on to ninth grade.

I was baffled. Why hadn't he flourished under my tutelage and Complex Instruction? Why wouldn't he participate? If student interaction increases learning, how could I have overcome Dennis's silence? How could I assign competence if he didn't do anything? What was my appropriate role in this kind of situation?

In hopes of finding answers to some of these questions, I decided to audiotape Dennis's group—and my interaction with it—during the Civil War unit. I intended to play it back when I had time to really listen and reflect.

The day I chose to tape had been a wild one. Thirty-two eighth graders were hunched in groups of four over resource cards that detailed the Civil War era. The classroom noise was at fever pitch as the students fired ideas back and forth nonstop, trying to choose a focus for their group projects.

As I moved from one group to the next, prodding, observing, and encouraging, I noticed that Dennis was not engaged with his group, which I had specially crafted with him in mind. Dennis had previously worked with two members of this foursome and I knew that if nominally pushed, both would be kind and try to include him. The fourth member, Tonesha, was a wild card. On any given day you didn't know whether she would be a social butterfly or a manic depressive. But on this particular day, it made little difference to Dennis, because he wasn't participating anyway. Instead, he sat slightly apart, fidgeting with a globe, which he used as a convenient barrier between himself and the rest of his group.

Frustrated, I went over and chided him, telling him to join his group. But he failed to respond, continuing simply to twirl the globe. Irritated, I moved his chair—with him in it—so there would be two students on each side of the table. Surely, I thought, the foursome would work better together if they all faced one another. I also moved the globe to an adjacent empty table.

"Dennis is in your group, too," I admonished the other three members, hoping to nudge them into trying to include Dennis despite their feeling that he was a "failure."

"We can't make him," mumbled Tonesha.

Inwardly I agreed. Outwardly I ignored her comment, since it could only lead us over old ground. I simply made my point and moved on.

The task of Dennis's group was to make a poster encouraging residents of Maryland, a border state, to join the Union rather than the Confederacy. At the moment, the students were working with resource cards. Unfortunately, when I subsequently returned to the group, I could see that these four students had not coalesced: Carmen and Tiffany were huddled over a resource card, but Tonesha was reading a list of songs from a Red Hot Chili Peppers tape and Dennis was staring into space, once again twirling the globe.

Frustration and disappointment rushed through me as I realized that despite my best efforts over the previous seven months, I'd been unable to help Dennis, to teach him, to touch him. He remained the lowest-status student in my class.

Trying to keep the edge from my voice, I addressed the girls: "Is Dennis a part of your group today?" Although Dennis piped up with "Yeah" and Carmen echoed him, I knew this was merely a ploy to send me on my way. I challenged Carmen, asking her directly, "How is he helping today?"

Dennis spoke up for himself. "I helped answer the questions." I knew that this was a charade, that he had done nothing. And I was stumped by the willingness of Carmen, Tonesha, and Tiffany to back up the lie. I wanted them to know that they had a responsibility to help get Dennis involved in their work. So I asked, "How are you helping him feel he's a part of your group?"

Dennis asserted himself again. Sounding almost as if he were trying to get the girls off the hook, he said more than I'd heard from him all year. "They're letting me discuss Carroll," he asserted. "They're talking about how she lived, and stuff."

I realized then that discussing Dennis's activity in the group would get me nowhere. I could almost feel myself deflate. So, with the demands of 28 other students pressing on me, I simply let go. I succumbed to the status quo called "Let's pretend Dennis is part of the group." Dennis and his fellow group members knew, as I did, that time was on their side, that I would eventually have to leave them to continue working with the other groups. But before leaving, I attempted to make eye contact with all four, asking, "Are you all feeling okay?" "Yeah," Carmen answered for the whole

group. I then asked if everyone had all the answers to their project questions and Carmen responded with a quiet, truthful no.

I then looked directly at Dennis, and in a last stab at pushing him toward the project, said, "Okay, make sure you all get them."

"I know," he responded with great assurance. But I knew that his answer was as empty as his folder, his portfolio, his binder.

Several months later, I began to reflect as I listened to the tape of that interaction. I had to listen three times before I realized what had really transpired that day—and a fourth time before glimpsing the implications of my role.

I had seen with my own eyes that Dennis wasn't engaged with the group. They had all lied to me about his involvement. I knew it was a lie, but hadn't confronted Dennis because I'd believed that he'd close down even further.

In a teacher-centered classroom, the withdrawn behavior of a student like Dennis is between him and the teacher. His fellow students are aware of the behavior, form opinions about him because of it, and may in turn reinforce his own low expectations of himself, but they are generally unaffected by his behavior. By contrast, in groupwork situations, a student's silence—Dennis's unhealthy invisible act—impacts his fellow students. They count on each other to help the group get a good grade, and one student's silence becomes a noticeable absence.

Believing that group expectations greatly affect the performance of its individual members, I had tried to stir the collective conscience of Dennis's teammates by asking what they were doing to make him a part of their group. It didn't help. In the end, it proved difficult to alter people's perceptions of Dennis, both his classmates' and his own—and, as I now realize, my own. We all participated in letting him remain aloof, and our collective failure to take responsibility for helping Dennis is itself immoral.

What became apparent during my fourth review of the audiotape was my own collaboration in Dennis's silence. I realized I had addressed the other members of the group as if Dennis were truly invisible. Instead of assigning competence, I did the opposite: I disembodied, objectified, and ultimately disempowered Dennis. No wonder the expectations of his peers were lower than I would have liked. In my own way I had unwittingly silenced him. I sealed and sanctioned room 20's unspoken understanding that "Dennis doesn't seem to be able to perform at an appropriate level; make room for him at your table; try and be kind."

The best intentions are not always enough to overcome the powerful model of teacher example. Dennis failed the last two marking periods as abysmally as the first four and did indeed fail eighth grade.

I had chosen to focus on Dennis with the hope that he would make a miraculous academic recovery if only I introduced groupwork and Complex Instruction. The fact that he didn't indicts neither groupwork generally nor Complex Instruction specifically. Groupwork offers all students, including ones like Dennis, many more immediate opportunities for academic participation than do more traditional forms of teaching. But no teaching method used as part of a social studies program for one academic year can turn every kid into an "A" student. Dennis's participation in some of the projects, while not enough, was positive and most likely more than his involvement in any other class. I like to think that if I'd had one more year with Dennis, I might have seen what I'd hoped for. But one year of Complex Instruction could not erase what had probably been an eight-year downward spiral.

Case 12

Learning to Listen to Robert

I believe each child teaches the teacher in new ways. After 10 months with Robert, I am still learning.

I teach a combination fifth–sixth grade science class in an urban elementary school with a large minority population. Robert, an African American child, came into my class as a new student several weeks after school started. He was large-bodied, slow-moving, and frequently late. He was also an excellent artist. Test scores from other schools revealed that Robert was a capable reader, and he never hesitated to speak up. Unfortunately, he always seemed to say just the wrong thing in just the wrong way.

Robert's speaking style was rapid and disjointed, and he sometimes stuttered. A typical sentence might be "I, I, I, I think, you know, I, I, what I think, I think that, you know, on TV, one time I was watching, TV, and, and then, I saw, I saw, you know, this kind of thing, this animal and it had a special way of protecting, you know, protecting itself." Although Robert seemed to know a lot about animals, it didn't take long before most of his fellow students grew impatient listening to him.

Delivery problems aside, many of Robert's comments seemed like non sequiturs, often leaving adults and children shaking their heads in confusion. For example, while the rest of the class concentrated on a science problem, Robert might easily announce that he had just received his new Nintendo. He seemed to have little sense of how to participate in sustained classroom conversation. This was a problem because in this classroom the act of talking, sharing thoughts, and exchanging meaning via dialogue was considered crucial to the deep exploration of content themes by children and teachers. Robert also spent a fair amount of time in his own little world. While other students talked, Robert often mumbled to himself or sang a quiet tune. Frequently he seemed unaware he was making these noises.

As a consequence of his idiosyncrasies, early on in the school year it seemed everything Robert said was either ignored or refuted by the other students—even when he was right. As one student said, "He just don't make any sense." As his teacher, I too was hard pressed to always know the relevance of the comments he offered or how they might fit into the ongoing conversation of the classroom. By late September it seemed clear that he had little status—with fellow students or his teachers. But I had hope for Robert.

After 12 years of teaching elementary school science and four years on the Brown/Campione research project, I have concluded that the child considered most irretrievable by others' standards might well shine when talking about and doing science. Over the years I have noticed that the child who doesn't do well socially or academically and who is regularly discussed at staff meetings may often set the stage for the most thoughtful discussions, both in the classroom and in the teachers' lounge. For years now I have been grappling with the notion that low-status children can drive classroom conversations in new and exciting directions, their provocative questions and comments taking teachers and fellow students into uncharted territory. As I considered Robert's status in the classroom, I realized that he offered a perfect opportunity to further examine these assumptions.

Early in October, immediately after one small group reciprocal teaching session about interdependence in the natural world, I began to suspect that there might be some important biological arguments buried in Robert's rambling and seemingly random comments. Robert belonged to a group of five students and one adult who were using reciprocal teaching* to discuss several pages

---

* Reciprocal Teaching (RT) was designed by Ann Marie Palincsar and Ann Brown in 1984. RT provides students with a set of cognitive strategies which enable the reader to have greater access and understanding of the text. Through a variety of questions first modeled by an adult, the child learns the importance of clarifying, predicting, summarizing, and interpreting newly revealed material. After seeing strategies modeled by an adult, students are encouraged to take turns being the "teacher." Eventually all RT groups are directed by the students themselves.

of a complex text that described the relationship between the use of DDT and the peregrine falcon's endangered species status. The aim was to have students develop a deep understanding of the important scientific theme of interdependence.

Throughout the discussion, Robert repeatedly tried to bring up the notion of using soap instead of a pesticide like Raid or DDT to kill insects. As usual, his ideas and words were disjointed: "If, if you tried to use soap, you know, to spray the plants with soap, you know, soap on the plants, the plants, you know, then, the DDT wouldn't be, you know, the soap and the bugs, the bugs would die... then there wouldn't, you wouldn't need no, no, no DDT or Raid." The children were confused, since this particular story mentioned neither bugs nor Raid. Instead, the text explained how DDT had affected falcons' eggs and the birds' reproductive capacity.

Both Lassie, a girl with keen intellect, acerbic verbal skills, and high social status, and Ron, a quick talker, strongly disagreed with everything Robert had to say. They responded to his comments with statements like "What are you talking about?" or "I just don't understand that." Nellie and Jennie remained quiet.

While talking, Robert had also been drawing in his notebook. He held it up saying, "See, see, it's here, the soap and the bugs...." He had drawn a short food chain with the peregrine at the top and the bugs (and the soap spray) near the bottom. With this drawing, he proved that he already understood the notion of interdependence, of toxic substances moving through the food chain. Robert understood the issue but was unable to convey that understanding to the others in his group. "What does soap have to do with falcons?" the children repeatedly asked. "*That's* not what we're reading."

Robert tried several times more to break into the discussion, but each time he was misunderstood and his comments were dismissed by the other students. All this happened so quickly that it was only in hindsight

that I could appreciate the complexity of Robert's reasoning. Near the end of that session, when I began to recognize where he might be heading, I tried to give Robert another chance, by asking more about his bug/soap theory: "Can you explain that some more to us?" But Robert still wasn't able to clearly articulate and link his ideas. His effort to let the drawings speak for him was unsuccessful, and his ideas were temporarily lost.

Upon later reflection, I realized that Robert's notions about alternatives to DDT and DDT's effects on the food chain were concepts that all the children could have profitably examined. By failing to explore these ideas we all had missed a golden opportunity.

I began to suspect that Robert had other worthy notions to contribute. But unless he was heard by other students, future opportunities would also be lost. Over the next few months, I listened very closely and came always to expect an original, but difficult to interpret, comment from Robert. I also saw that because of his low status, Robert was becoming increasingly invisible. He was beginning to speak less frequently in small group discussions.

I began to look for ways to capitalize on Robert's words. Theorizing that a certain percentage of his ideas might help generate high-level discussion, I decided that if necessary I would actively intervene so his ideas could be heard by other students. I waited for an opportunity to present itself.

In December, two months after the group discussion about DDT and falcons, the same group of five students discussed aquatic animals that are harmed or made extinct by DDT and other habitat disruptions. Nellie had asked for help in deciphering an article on fish extinction, and in the middle of the discussion, Robert interrupted with a loud, "I got it."

In his typically garbled syntax, he offered an idea. "They should get some fish genes and then get some plant genes—then they mix them up and then it would be a fish-plant—then they couldn't be harmed by DDT." He followed this statement with a convoluted story about eggplant mutation. The rest of the group was surprised—and confused. Ron said, "I think he's trying to say that fish genes should be mixed with plant genes so DDT wouldn't harm them."

No one picked up on the comment and the conversation shifted back to Nellie's original question. She was confused, in part, about the term "rediscovery" as applied to a rare species of pupfish thought to be extinct. I explained that scientists can't "rediscover" a species that is truly extinct, but that if a small number of that species happened to be living undetected in a remote area, they could someday be "rediscovered." I mentioned that this had, in fact, happened with several species that biologists had once thought to be extinct. Just after this explanation, Robert loudly chimed in, "Oh, I get it, oh, I get it... you said you can't discover the same thing, that's what you're saying, like if they died you can't rediscover the same fish. Yeah."

Robert's comments revealed his understanding of a difficult concept. I quickly realized that we might be teetering on the edge of a discussion that might lead to deeper biological principles. Because I had learned an important lesson from the soap/DDT reciprocal teaching interaction, this time I decided to seize the moment, unwilling to let a potentially rich conversation die for lack of encouragement. I made a quick decision to redirect the discussion to Robert's gene theory, in an attempt to get to the heart of his meaning. I knew there might not be gold in Robert's words but decided that it was worth the gamble.

I temporarily resumed teacher control of the small group by asking Robert to further explain his original fish-plant gene idea. So Robert explained, "It's like, you know, it's like you got the genes of your momma and daddy, you know what your momma and daddy give you so, like, the genes of your ears are from your momma or your daddy, that's who you got them from." Happily, other students, especially Lassie, also wanted to talk about genes. Listening to Robert, they were saying "Oh" and "Yeah" in unison. Lassie interrupted, saying, "Like my Mom has gray eyes, so I might get my gray eyes from my Mom. That would be a gene, right?" The other group members again said, "Yeah."

As a group we had begun to negotiate meaning for the word "gene," using Robert's original fish-gene "thought experiment" as raw material for discussion. The group would need to negotiate and refine that meaning over time, yet this was an auspicious beginning and Robert had brought us here.

In his comment "I think he's trying to say..." Ron had attempted to reinterpret Robert's original suggestion. In doing so, Ron had emphasized the importance of Robert's notions, giving them status for the rest of the group. The same thing occurred when Robert and Lassie together explored the meaning of the term "gene."

In fact, the children had all helped teach each other, but the original impetus had come from Robert. And the actual negotiation of meaning had occurred only after the discussion had slowed down enough so that children actually listened to each other, especially to the seemingly strange notion of fish-plant genes. By actively intervening, I had changed the group process so that other children had to consider Robert's solution. Because I intervened, one unlikely child brought a certain content richness to a small group discussion.

While talking with and listening to the group, I was aware that we had achieved a significant breakthrough, and I was gratified that Robert's comments took the group on an important side trip to genetics. This event verified my belief that low-status children can propel discourse to new and exciting terrain, given the opportunity. While I never can predict the exact content or time of the interaction, I could be relatively certain that such a conversation would eventually take place. Robert had elevated, rather than dragged down, the discussion and thus led five other students to a new level of questioning.

I would like to say that this event turned everything around for Robert, and that students subsequently valued his comments, but this is not the case. One successful session did not solve longstanding problems. Things improved, but it was still a struggle. Months after the fish-gene episode, Robert's group still most often ignores his repeated "I know, I know."

Subsequent small group sessions were firm reminders that guiding equal access to dialogue to all children, but especially low achievers, would be a continuing struggle and that small victories could be obliterated. Because I had seen how Robert had enriched several discussions while children were engaged in deep and challenging content areas, I continue to work toward leveling the playing field so that all students could participate fully.

Yet because I want students to take maximal ownership of their own learning, the line between student and teacher direction must shift constantly in creative and flexible ways. I am left with questions that strongly influence my teaching practice and subsequent reliance on the theory that underpins practice. First among these questions is how a teacher can know when a potentially rich content area and its accompanying social interactions warrant intervention. Just how much will be "enough," understanding fully that both social skills and content knowledge will increase over time so that less intervention eventually will be necessary? Inquiry into these areas requires time, patience, and new insights into group process. Students like Robert show the way.

I believe cooperative groups are most effective when the students engage in rich complex activities, learning by doing. I also believe they learn more when the teacher's role is to facilitate learning instead of just imparting information. Yet when my students do groupwork, I always struggle with the same dilemmas: if and when to intervene, and how to ensure that low-status students actively participate and high-status students do not dominate.

Thirty percent of the students at our school are Hispanic, many bused from other neighborhoods to attend our bilingual program. Most of our native Spanish-speaking families are originally from small communities in Mexico; the parents are migrant workers and the families move with the growing season. Few of these families speak English, and most have very low reading and writing skills, even in their native language.

I taught in Mexico for three years before moving to the United States and becoming a bilingual teacher. Because I went through some adjustments myself, I have been able to relate to the struggles of my Spanish-speaking students as they search for their place in this new culture. From the beginning I planned a lot of cooperative activities that would allow students to interact regardless of their language ability. This way everyone could learn from each other.

Whenever we do groupwork, I choose activities complex enough to require many different abilities. To complete a task, a group needs students skilled in reading and writing, but also those with other abilities, such as balancing, building, drawing, estimating, hypothesizing, and measuring. Every member of the group can use at least one of his abilities and can contribute to completion of the task. Each student plays a specific role in the group: facilitator, checker, reporter, or safety monitor. Task instructions are always provided on activity cards in both English and Spanish, and in each group one student serves as translator.

I use specific strategies to encourage students to use their many abilities and to recognize them for doing so. For example, I observe them as they work in groups and give very specific and public feedback. I also show how what they've done is critical to the task at hand and how they contributed to their group.

The groupwork has by and large been very successful. At the beginning of the school year, there are always some academically weak students who are clearly considered outsiders by their classmates. By the end of the year, however, most have developed a sense of belonging. They have become active participants in their work groups and begun to demonstrate more self-esteem.

But one year, one particular low-status student in my third grade bilingual class showed no signs of being integrated into his group. He just had too many problems to overcome.

Miguel was a shy and withdrawn child who spoke no English and stuttered when he spoke Spanish. His Spanish reading and writing skills were very low, and although math was his strength, nobody seemed to notice. Recently arrived from a small community in Mexico, Miguel lived with relatives—more than 10 adults and three children in a two-bedroom apartment. He came to school hungry and tired, and wearing dirty clothes. Shunned by his classmates, who said he had the "cooties," Miguel was left out of group activities. Even when he had a specific role, other members of the group would take over and tell him what to do. Miguel was obviously a low-status student.

When I observed Miguel's group I saw that the other members simply wouldn't give him a chance. Cooperative learning was not helping him at all. Miguel grew more isolated by the day. Students increasingly teased him, and he was getting into fights and becoming a behavior problem. I realized the only way to change students' views about Miguel was to show them that he had certain abilities to contribute to his group. My challenge was to identify his strengths and show his peers that he was competent.

One day in May, we were working in cooperative groups building different structures with straws, pins, clay, and wires. I was observing Miguel's group and saw him quietly pick up some straws and pins and start building a structure following the diagram on one of the activity cards. The other members of the group were trying to figure out how to begin their structure, and as usual, were not paying much attention to Miguel. I observed that Miguel had used double straws to make the base more sturdy. He knew exactly what to do because he had looked at the diagram on the card. In other words, Miguel knew that the task was to build as sturdy a structure as possible, and he understood the principle of making the base stronger by using double straws.

I knew that this was the chance I was waiting for; it was clear that Miguel had the ability to build things by following diagrams. I decided to intervene, speaking both Spanish and English, since not everyone in the group spoke Spanish. I told the group that Miguel understood the task very well and would be an important resource because he had a great ability to construct something by looking at the diagram. I also said that Miguel might grow up to be an architect since building sturdy structures by following diagrams is one of the things architects need to do. I also told the group they had to rely on their translator so Miguel could explain what he was doing.

I continued observing the group from a distance, and sure enough, a few minutes later the translator was asking Miguel for help. Miguel explained to the members of his group what he had done and why. It was obvious he had abilities that could help him succeed in cooperative learning groups, and his group finally realized it. But I wanted everyone in the classroom to know that Miguel was very good at building structures.

So when his group reported on their work, I said I had noticed that they had some problems understanding the task, and I asked their reporter what had helped them complete the task successfully.

He told the class that Miguel had understood what to do and had explained it to the group. I then reinforced the reporter's explanation, adding that Miguel had shown competence in building things by looking at a diagram and that his contribution had helped his group solve the problem successfully. By assigning competence to Miguel in front of his group and the whole class, I made sure everyone knew that Miguel had a lot to contribute to his peers. This was a wonderful example for everyone of how important it is to explore the multiple abilities of all group members in completing the task. After this, things changed for Miguel. His group members not only recognized him as an active member but began using him as a resource to help them balance their structures.

Miguel's status changed after my intervention, but I am convinced that had I recognized his competence earlier in the year and given him specific feedback, his school year would have been much improved. The experience raised a number of questions for me. Why hadn't I taken the time to observe Miguel's performance earlier in the year so he could have been viewed as a resource both in groupwork and in other areas? Had I somehow been convinced he had no abilities? What would have happened if I hadn't been observing during those few seconds when Miguel was building his structure and no one was aware of what he was doing? Would Miguel have continued to be ignored totally by his peers? How long would it have taken for someone to realize that Miguel is a capable boy? What happens to students like Miguel who have abilities no one knows about? Will they ever be successful? Sometimes I feel I don't see what's right in front of me and tend to have low expectations for low-status students, forgetting that the less we expect, the less students give.

Miguel is not at my school anymore, but I have heard he is doing well. He still has problems, but he has more friends and is getting better grades. I want to think that some of his success was because of my intervention.

C. INTERACTIONS WITH PARENTS AND COLLEAGUES

Case 14

An Extra Audience of Critics: Handling a Parent's Response

I am an intern teacher in the social studies department of a high school in an upscale San Francisco suburb. For a variety of reasons, I feel especially fortunate to have received this particular placement. Discipline is rarely an issue because students have been socialized to obey, respect, and trust their elders. The social studies department is close knit and its members mutually supportive. My colleagues are sensitive to the demands of the education courses I take in conjunction with my teaching assignment. And because I have only one prep, I have more time to plan and learn the content of my curriculum.

My school also has an involved and well-educated parent population. Ironically, it has proved to be a mixed blessing. Most of the parents have advanced degrees; they have their own ideas about teaching and are quite vocal about how things should or shouldn't be taught.

I learned this firsthand when I was wrapping up a unit on the Renaissance in which I had concentrated on the intellectual concepts that distinguish the Renaissance from the Middle Ages. To conclude the unit, I devised a group project called Living Art, which asked students to draw connections between Renaissance art and the major intellectual themes of the period.

I divided the class into six groups and assigned each a Renaissance art masterpiece about which they would become experts. The project included three tasks: (1) as a group, research the assigned painting and its artist; (2) as an individual, write a report that analyzes the work and explains how it portrays Renaissance ideas and values; and (3) as a group, use costumes, props, and a backdrop to pose as your painting, and at the same time, present the information found in the research, noting the themes in particular.

To evaluate the assignment, I planned to have the other students assess the accuracy of each group's pose, backdrop, costumes, and props while I graded the individual reports, the students' ability to work as a group, and the content of the presentation.

I created this assignment because I had learned in my education courses that students have a better chance of internalizing conceptual information when it is presented through visual and kinesthetic learning activities. In theory, this type of assignment engages more students than a traditional reading- and writing-based assignment because a wider range of abilities is required for successful completion of the project. I had hoped this assignment would encourage my students who have difficulty reading and writing to participate because it offered them a chance to shine in nontraditional ways. I was soon to find out that some did not agree with my methods.

The first day went according to plan, with all the students working diligently on their research and sharing information among themselves surprisingly well. The second day began smoothly. The students worked hard on their individual reports. (I had imposed testlike conditions to convey the importance of the report.) During the second half of the period, when the groups met to plan the pose and presentation, things were a lot more chaotic. Within their groups, students had difficulty listening to each other and getting organized. Some groups struggled to decide whether to tackle first the pose or the creation of the backdrop. Personality conflicts that might seem subtle in a teacher-centered classroom were amplified in this setting.

I found it hard to watch all this. I realize now that as a teacher I find it uncomfortable to relinquish control. But in order for students to learn the skills necessary for successful groupwork, I felt I had to let them argue and otherwise work out conflicts on their own.

For this assignment, group size depended on the number of characters in the painting. Because one slide I selected, da Vinci's "St. Anne and the Virgin," has only two figures, one group comprised just two students. I chose Sara and Samantha, best friends who are both accomplished, motivated, and mature students. Although I had conceived the assignment as an in-class project, I made special allowances when these two asked to work on their backdrop at home over the weekend. I never considered the extra audience of critics that would be there to supervise the work of the two girls.

On the last day of the assignment, the poses and presentations went very well. My adviser and the department chair observed and were impressed with the complexity of the reports and the pride students took in posing. Students brought in elaborate costumes and took the posing very seriously; I think peer grading of poses gave them added incentive to strive for excellence. The students also made impressive connections between the paintings and general Renaissance themes. The general level of artistic analysis was, in my opinion, college level, with students discussing such things as the use of perspective, sfumato, chiaroscuro, and controposto— terms used to describe painting techniques. Sara, for instance, told the class that until she had tried to pose as St. Anne next to the Virgin Mary, she hadn't noticed how inaccurately da Vinci had used scale. Only when trying to recreate the painting's pose with her group partner did Sara realize that in real life a human arm would not be able to extend across Mary's body as it had in the painting.

In this project I felt I had achieved my goals. Even students who were typically underachievers were actively engaged. I also felt the students made the connection between Italian Renaissance art and the larger themes that characterize this period in history. As a beginning teacher, I had rarely experienced teaching success, but at the end of this assignment I felt a rare sense of euphoria. It wasn't to last.

The project concluded on a Tuesday. After the students finished their presentations, I debriefed them. On Wednesday, I began instruction on the next chapter, the Reformation. No problem.

Friday came, and with it a problem. As the first bell rang that morning, Sara approached with an odd grin, handing me a sealed envelope. "Here, Ms. M.," she said, "This is for you." I put it aside and began the class. It wasn't until afterward, when I was alone, that I sat down to read the letter. Although I opened it with the curiosity of a child opening a gift, the single-page letter signed by Sara's father proved less than a welcome present:

Dear Ms. M.,

Last weekend, Sammi [Samantha] and my daughter Sara spent some time with paper, slide projector, pastels, and tape, drawing the background for what I'm told would be an in-class pose of one of da Vinci's work. My first thought was: "How sweet." My second thought, once I realized that the first thought was only appropriate for a grade school project, was: "What is this for?"

Now both kids assured me that the posing is in conjunction with a report on Leonardo and serves as additional material. However, they did mention that posing and drawing was assigned, not optional.

Now, I remember hokey stuff like that from my own elementary school days several hundred years ago: a quiz show featuring food, clothing, and shelter of Peru.

But this is high school. Are the kids incapable of learning without entertainment? Or is this a clever scheme so that when the subject of art comes up in twenty years, something will immediately spring to mind? Or perhaps the problem is that there's not enough material to teach in this year's social studies class? In other words, did someone really suggest this as a curriculum write-up? And did you believe it?

Do I misunderstand? Were the kids staging an elaborate hoax on an impressionable parent to make him believe that there's so much time in the school year that you have the liberty to engage in this crap?

I feel obliged to say that the last letter I wrote to a teacher was about algebra, and the issues that came up when my daughter and I discussed it. It didn't flame in this manner. But then again, algebra's the real stuff. So is social studies. Just not the fluff.

Call me if you wish. I'll apologize, and you can set me straight if I have the story wrong. But it sure looks grim from here.

With one fell swoop, that letter wiped out all the satisfaction I felt about the Living Art project. I was shocked at its angry, sarcastic tone, thinking I must have done something dreadfully wrong to elicit such a scathing response from a parent. Sara happens to be one of my strongest students, and I thought we had a good relationship. After reading her father's letter, I completely reevaluated our relationship. Understandably, the letter also caused me to rethink the Living Art assignment and groupwork in general.

As an intern teacher, I lack the experience to have solid confidence in my ability to teach, choose materials, and create assignments. This attack destroyed what confidence I had. In its place I had only questions.

With only a few months of training under my belt, who am I to decide what these students should learn? And how can I expect parents with at least 20 years more life experience than me to trust my ability to choose the curriculum for their children's social science education in their first impressionable year of high school? Teachers have used traditional reading and writing methods of instruction for years; who am I to think that the use of visual and kinesthetic learning will be better? Is this parent right? Was the Living Art assignment merely an effort to entertain these MTV-generation students?

Were the thematic connections I sought manufactured in my mind to ease my own doubts about this unorthodox assignment?

I have since graded the unit test on the Renaissance and the Reformation. As part of the test, students had been asked to write a short essay analyzing Raphael's "The School of Athens" and explaining how this particular painting epitomizes Renaissance art. The essays were wonderful. The students analyzed the technical aspects of this complicated work like college students, rather than high school freshmen. More important, almost all of the students were able to relate the painting to the larger complex concepts of the Renaissance.

Should I be happy with this result, or did they merely jump through the hoops I'd set up for them? Did they learn anything valuable? Sara's father made a point of recalling his own teacher's "hokey" assignment when his class was studying Peru. Yet some 30 years later, he still remembers that "hokey" assignment. Is this bad? Isn't the goal of education, at least to some degree, for students to internalize and retain information? Isn't that what happened for Sara's dad as a result of the Peru assignment? As a teacher, I would be delighted if some of my students actually remembered how to analyze Renaissance art 30 years from now as a result of my Living Art project.

I suppose I should take solace in the fact that *all* of my students were actively involved in the project with no prodding from me. I received quality test essays, even from those who usually have problems on traditional assessments. I am satisfied with the value of kinesthetic assignments and will incorporate them in the future. These outcomes seem to corroborate arguments that multiple-ability tasks reach more students than those that fit the verbal learning style category. However, they do not at all satisfy the *parent* who is a verbal learner.

Yet questions still float in my head for which I have no answers. I know that throughout her career, a teacher is bound to encounter some resistance to her teaching methods, but I never envisioned it happening during my intern year. I also know people aren't going to treat me with kid gloves just because I'm new at this and my ego is fragile, nor should they. But the fact remains that I am afraid to assign multiple-ability groupwork tasks again. Truthfully, I am nervous about exploiting students' kinesthetic, visual, and auditory learning skills and styles. The bottom line is that I was not prepared to face such an ardent challenge to my teaching philosophy so early in its development. Whether it warrants such reflection or not, the letter from Sara's father has caused me to question the very foundation of my teaching philosophy.

I composed a brief letter in response to this disgruntled parent, trying to be as professional as possible. (My letter had to be approved by my cooperating teacher and the department chair before I sent it out.) I felt no responsibility to justify my actions to this man. Moreover, I felt an attempt at justification would only give credence to his accusations. I believe any constructive criticism his letter may have contained was lost in its malicious and unprofessional tone. I believe my own response proved two points: that I am a true professional and that I stick to my choice of curriculum and assignments despite adversity. I wrote:

> *Dear Mr. M.,*
>
> *I received your letter on Friday of last week. It is unfortunate that we have different opinions on the instruction of Italian Renaissance ideas and values through art. However, I appreciate your effort in airing your questions and criticisms. While it is never easy to accept criticism, as a teacher I am encouraged by any parent who takes an active interest in the education of his or her child.*

> *I maintained definite goals and clear reasons for choosing to assign the art project, many of which are supported by pedagogical theory and research. However, a letter is not the proper format in which curriculum and instruction ought to be discussed. If you are concerned or interested, please feel free to contact me again through the history department. I would be happy to continue the dialogue.*

If nothing else, writing this letter was therapeutic for me. I doubt it appeased Sara's father—and I'm not sure that I care. I got what I needed, a sense of closure on the experience.

Case 15

Walking the Talk: Cooperative Learning for Teachers

As part of my training in a new collaborative mathematics project, I attend monthly in-service sessions where experienced teachers instruct us on how to teach each unit. The teachers model the activities and we neophytes act as students, experiencing what the students will go through as they do various activities.

In the training, we are seated in groups of four and given the activities and manipulatives needed to complete each activity. It is assumed that because we are adults, we know how to make our group productive and harmonious and that we don't need roles or group skillbuilders to help us function as a group.

I'm beginning to have doubts about the teachers who are training us in this wonderful new collaborative curriculum. It's assumed that adults can function in groups since they are mature, understanding, and experienced—but the following case presents a situation where they are not. How can these teachers fix status problems in their classrooms when they can't fix them in their own groups? What is being done to train these teachers to see their own problems, which in turn can help them see problems in their classrooms?

Even though I was a young student teacher when this case took place, I knew that both students and adults need to be taught the necessary behaviors, attitudes, and rules for collaborative groupwork. I was simultaneously taking a collaborative groupwork class at Stanford University, where we discussed strategies and status problems. The discussions tested my ability to apply strategies to the status problems that occurred at my in-service training.

I was grouped with three teachers: two were white males from a local high school, and the third was an African American female from another high school. I'd worked with all three in past sessions and knew them pretty well. Jerry is a department head, and he is mathematically powerful. He really knows his math

and lets everyone know that fact. He is a bit stuffy and aloof and likes to work alone rather than cooperatively. Bob is Jerry's foil; his knowledge of mathematics doesn't seem to come close to Jerry's. But Bob is friendly and has a good rapport with everyone at the in-service group. Dotty teaches math but won't teach our particular project until next year. Like Bob, Dotty does not seem to know the mathematics that is going on in the units. When I work in groups with her, she doesn't contribute a lot of quality to the discussion or activities; she is just there. So I feel as if I'm getting taken for a ride—it's the so-called sucker effect.

At the in-service sessions, the teachers usually give us an outline of the unit which details what mathematical concepts are being taught. This time, they turned the tables on us and gave us the task of making the outline ourselves. But the task had a bit of a twist; instead of going through the unit and outlining it, we were assigned to search out the activities and homework assignments that pertained to the concept of similarity in triangles. These activities and homework assignments consisted of two groups: one addressed the *students' intuition and prior knowledge of what makes triangles similar,* and the second stressed the *mathematical manipulation of equations dealing with ratios and similar triangles.* For the entire morning, we were to find these activities and homework assignments and place them in their proper groups. Then we were to discuss how these activities would engage the students in building an understanding of similar triangles. After lunch, we were to present our findings to the entire class.

With our task in mind, my group decided to leaf through our teacher's manuals individually to find the activities and homework assignments in question. Later we would get together to see how we agreed and discuss how these assignments would engage the students and build their understanding. With that strategy in mind, we individually searched for the appropriate activities in our teacher's manuals.

Jerry demanded quiet so his train of thought would not be broken. Bob read and asked me for help, then read some more and talked some more. Dotty went page by page and started to outline selected parts of the unit.

When we got together as a group to see if we agreed on which activities were for intuition and which were for manipulation, we didn't get off to the best possible start. Jerry said he needed more time. Bob said he had a general idea of which activities were for intuition and which were for manipulation, but he really hadn't thought about how they engaged the students. Dotty produced a massive outline of some of the activities for the unit but did not identify which ones tested students' intuition and knowledge of similarity and which exercised mathematical manipulation. Her outline detailed what the assignments were and what they stressed, but she failed to group them as assigned. I had an idea of where the mini-unit on similarity started and ended and where there was a transition from intuition to mathematical manipulation of ratios, so I was okay. The in-service leaders checked our progress and looked at our individual products. They asked us to meld our work for our group presentation.

During our next stage, the discussion of how the assignments would engage students and build understanding, Dotty got the impression her outline was not valuable to us. She felt we dismissed her piece as not pertinent to our task and a waste of time. Although we did not say outright that her work was a waste of time, I think she got that impression through our body language and by our focusing on our work. Dotty began a tirade; she remarked that she thought she had done what was asked of the group, but now we were doing something totally different. She ended with the remark, "I just get the idea that everybody thinks I'm dumb. I know I ain't teaching this like you all are doing now, but I ain't that dumb." She put her outline away, reached into her bookbag, took out a Book-of-the-Month Club romance novel, and started to read. I tried to ask her what she thought was wrong with our group, but Jerry

patted me on the arm and put his fingers to his lips to get me to stop trying to talk to her. I guess he just wanted us to let her be.

Dotty went away to cool off. The rest of us tried to get back on task because time was running out. Lunch was nearing and we had to get our presentation ready for after lunch. We didn't even try to discuss what had got Dotty so ticked off. Instead, we acted as if nothing big had happened. When Dotty got back, Bob asked if we had made her angry. She said we had, and Bob tried to comfort her by saying that he too felt dumb at our in-service sessions. I wanted to intervene and say that we weren't trying to make anyone feel dumb, that we were all there to help, but before I could say anything, Jerry started urging us to complete the task. I wanted to fix the problem before anything else big exploded in our faces, but Jerry just wanted to get the project done.

We finished the project, but we looked awful. Dotty presented her outline, which did not answer the central question of how we were to engage students. Bob stumbled his way through an explanation of how the activities worked off students' intuition. Jerry presented a very articulate discussion of the mathematical approach to similarity, and I bulled my way through the algebra of proportion, ratio, and similarity. We seemed like four parts rather than a group, and you could tell we were really disjointed. We did not produce a coherent effort.

Even with adults there are status problems. Jerry feels he is of high status (as do the rest of the teachers) due to the mathematical skill and knowledge he has shown during our in-service sessions. Bob works with Jerry and feels inferior to him and the rest of the class. Bob feels he is not 100% a math teacher, since he splits his efforts between teaching math and coaching sports. Dotty feels out of the loop because she doesn't teach the curriculum yet and therefore can't relate to our experiences and feelings about it. I see myself as competent— and, because of my classes at Stanford, a step ahead of my colleagues when it comes to making groupwork work. I don't think any of them has taken classes or attended training sessions on cooperative learning. I don't feel as mathematically powerful as Jerry, but I feel that my experience and knowledge about groupwork puts me on an even keel with him.

What would I have done differently to treat the status problems in this group? The first step would have been for us to communicate to each other our thoughts and feelings on how we felt about our group's interactions. Even though discussing it would have taken time away from our task, I think it would have been valuable for us as professionals to talk it out. By not talking, I felt that the problem was unresolved and could have grown bigger. I myself deferred to Jerry's higher status in the group and failed to intervene. In retrospect, I would exercise my right as a group member to fix the problem rather than sweep it under the rug, hoping it would not creep out from underneath. By not intervening, I too was a victim of the status problems in my group.

I wanted to treat the status problem in our group but I didn't. Why didn't I try? Was it because I was the youngest one and thought my inexperience would not do any good? Was it because as the class clown I thought nothing I said or did would be taken seriously? Was it because the group's notion that a problem will go away if you leave it alone overpowers my idea that you need to treat the problem before it grows into a cancer?

I was really disappointed that adults who train young students on the benefits of groupwork couldn't function as group members in a training session. We are in charge of treating status problems in the classroom and we can't even fix our own. Intervening and trying to treat the problem was seen by Jerry as exacerbating it. When he prevented me from trying to fix the problem, he gave me the impression that if we didn't do any-thing, it would magically disappear. I wonder what Jerry does in his class when these types of problems crop up. Does he tell the students to be quiet and that the problem will go away if you don't talk about it or confront it?

The curriculum leaders for this project need to be aware that we are not perfect teachers and we have problems treating status levels in our classrooms. I have told them that they have to teach us how to use cooperative groups and that this skill doesn't come naturally for us or for the kids. I hope the summer training session I'll be going to will confront the subject of cooperative learning in the classroom. This will make us more aware of what is going on in our classrooms, and even more, in our own groups during training sessions.

CHAPTER 3

One Teacher's Odyssey

This final chapter portrays one teacher's year-long struggle to incorporate a particular model of groupwork into her classroom. In this comprehensive narrative, the author examines how this model differs from other approaches to groupwork and why it is appealing. Yet she also explores why some students appeared to flourish in collaborative activities and not others, and when her actions appeared to advance or hinder the process. This case addresses many of the questions that are raised in earlier cases, thus it can serve as an introduction to or synthesis of the range of complex issues teachers face when they attempt to make collaborative groupwork an integral part of their pedagogical repertoire.

Case 16

We're All in This Together

Christi probably wants to be a teacher when she grows up. I can tell by the way she enjoys having authority, organizing others, being the expert. I see a lot of myself in her. Yet suddenly this child who had never given me any problems is throwing tantrums and creating turmoil.

What's happening to Christi?

For years I had used cooperative learning in my seventh grade core class, a combined language arts and social studies program. Groupwork was useful at times when I needed some distance, but mostly I used it because it was the trend and it added variety to my teaching repertoire. I didn't think much about whether groupwork might actually help kids learn better. I thought the social interaction was good for them and that the change of pace would be okay for the academics, too. But in truth, I believed that all their real learning in my class had to be filtered through me.

What *I* really enjoyed about being a teacher was my interaction with the kids. I liked getting to know them individually and watching their personalities emerge and develop as they encountered new challenges and ideas. What was most important to me was the kind of bonding that occurred as we moved through the year developing trust, and openness, and love… yet still getting on with the business of learning something about the curriculum.

Although groupwork was never a really high priority for me, whenever I did use it, I wanted it to go well. Most often I was disappointed. Much of what I had kids do in groups could just as easily and more efficiently have been done independently, so one or two students were always taking over the group while the rest coasted.

My attempt to fix this problem resulted in larger tasks, with assignments so detailed and lengthy that one or two students couldn't possibly complete them alone.

This kept everybody busy during class, and at first I was pleased with the way they divided up the labor. But some groups fell apart under the sheer weight of the workload, and in others I noticed that nearly every day the same students said, "That's okay, I'll take it home and finish it." Christi was always one such student, and when presentation time came it was usually she who had the most to say.

In terms of real cooperative learning, I was beginning to think that groupwork was just one more great idea that never quite worked. But because I thought the development of social skills was important, I kept looking for a way to make it better. Eventually I became involved with Complex Instruction.*

Learning about multiple intellectual abilities redefined my ideas about the nature of group tasks and gave me a new curriculum that engaged students in exciting ways. It required everyone in the group to pool resources in order to investigate difficult primary source evidence and to present findings in creative, engaging ways. These problem solving tasks were designed to be multidimensional and open-ended so that no one could successfully complete them alone. This increasing interdependence seemed to pull the rug right out from under Christi's sense of security.

The first of the new activities was an introductory unit on poetry. Christi, Roberto, LaToya, and Raymond were studying sound and rhythm in poetry. After looking at a painting by Breughel and reading William Carlos Williams's poem "The Dance," they were to discuss the sense of motion in the poem and how it was created. Then they were to choose from several other pictures and create their own lines of poetry, bringing out the sounds and rhythm of the activities in the one they chose.

---

* Complex Instruction, developed at Stanford University, is a groupwork model that emphasizes the development of higher-order thinking skills in heterogeneous classrooms. It addresses issues of status that arise in small groups.

Christi and Raymond were locked in serious argument over which picture to choose. LaToya preferred a third picture and seemed willing to negotiate. Roberto pushed back his desk and shrugged. Heated words and hard feelings abounded. I intervened with some conflict resolution strategies and a compromise was reached, but it wasn't long until they were at it again.

"You can't just sit there," Christi commanded Roberto. "You have to tell us which one you want. Ms. Knight says we all have to discuss and you've gotta say which one you want!"

Roberto just smiled and shrugged. It was not a shrug of ignorance or even indifference. It was meant to placate, to show he'd go along, give way. It is the only comment Roberto ever makes. He entered this class at the beginning of the second quarter from the bilingual core class after his bilingual teacher said his English skills were good enough for him to be in regular classes. "Roberto certainly has some problems with reading and writing at grade level, but his general comprehension is pretty good," she said. Yet Roberto has done no work in six weeks and is failing in both English and social studies. He smiles and shrugs often, but his gray eyes are lively and he watches everything. Sometimes he can barely suppress his interest.

Now Roberto is under attack. Raymond and LaToya are tired of sparring with Christi, and all three of them have joined in haranguing Roberto for not participating. They have picked up the lingo pretty well.

"Everybody has to participate."

"None of us are as smart as all of us together."

"If we don't all contribute, then we can't really do a good job."

"Come on, Roberto, you have to talk about this with us."

"Ms. Knight, Roberto won't participate!"

They've forgotten about their own differences and focused their collective frustration on Roberto. The task is difficult and uncertain; there is no single clear right answer; they're not sure what to do or how to do it; and time is getting shorter and shorter. It must be somebody's fault. Raymond, LaToya, and Christi are all B students, so they figure it can't be their fault; it must be Roberto's! For Christi the situation is especially painful. She is out of her seat, fidgety with anxiety and frustration. She slaps her desk for emphasis.

I join the group. Having already overheard some of the complaints from a distance, I deliberately turn to Roberto, asking, "What seems to be the problem?"

"Ms. Knight, he won't do anything," Christi intrudes. "He won't say anything. He just sits there." I hear the rising whine in her voice and then the sob. "And you say that the group is responsible for everyone participating. So now we're all gonna get a bad grade and…."

Now there are tears and Raymond and LaToya are nodding. I'm wondering if this is worth it and why good students should have to put up with this. This just looks like more of the same old thing and I want to yell at them all.

But I'm aware that around the room most of the other groups are productively engaged. So, calming myself, I say, "What do you think about this, Roberto?"

He shrugs and looks down at his hands as he fiddles with his pencil. There are no smiles now.

"Do you understand why they are upset with you?" I ask. He nods. "Tell me why you think they're upset with you," I say.

He shrugs. I wait.

Christi starts to speak. I put my hand on her arm.

We're All in This Together

We all wait.

Then it comes. Haltingly, softly, in lightly accented, clear English, "They say I don't talk enough."

"Do you think that's true?"

A shrug, then a nod yes.

"It sounds like your group really needs you and really wants your ideas. What would make it easier for you to talk more in your group?"

A very long pause. "If they don't yell."

I turn to the other three. "Okay, how about if you agree not to yell anymore and to give Roberto some time to answer?" I suggest. "Then you really try to listen to him." Christi is still sullen and anxious, but all three nod.

"And what are you going to do, Roberto?" I ask.

He looks up with that familiar smile. "Talk more," he says.

After all that trauma, Christi and Roberto's group really doesn't have time to finish the project, and when presentations come, they don't have much to show or tell. I talk with them and the class about what happened in their group and about their breakthrough. But at the same time, I worry about using two class periods with so little to show for them.

Other groups are more successful. Lori and Leo's group read Gwendolyn Brooks's poem "We Real Cool" aloud and then perform their own composition—a rap about war, complete with all the elements of pattern and repetition that they've investigated in their activity. I am surprised and impressed.

We don't work in groups every day, and by the time we get back to the poetry activities a few days later, I have pretty much forgotten about the incident in Christi's group. But eventually I become aware that there have been no outbursts from that corner of the room. Instead, there's that definite hum of on-task conversation. I saunter over to observe.

"How's it going?" I ask.

They hardly pause, but there are nods and hums of response.

"Everybody participating?" I know I should leave them alone, but I press for more.

"How's it going for you today, Roberto?"

I am rewarded with a smile and a nod. "It's good," he says.

I was confident that this group's serious problems were resolved, and I was comfortable with the progress of the other groups as well. They were all beginning to buzz along more productively but still testing me occasionally to see if they really did have the authority to make their own decisions.

They wanted to do well. No one wanted to get up in front of the class and look like a fool. They were catching on, and the changes in some of the students were surprising.

Roberto was one who had made much improvement. He spoke up more frequently, and as I pointed out the value of his contributions, others in the class began to take his opinions more seriously. He was by no means a great student, but he was no longer failing.

Roberto's progress was especially noticeable when Miguel returned after four months in Mexico. When the two boys came into the class together from bilingual core, Miguel was an eager student who chided Roberto for his bad grades. Now Miguel was completely lost and Roberto was his instructor. As Roberto taught Miguel the group process, I heard him say, "You gotta talk. Everybody gotta participate or your group don't do so good."

Of course, there remained all the other regular classwork to do in language arts and social studies; we still explored each unit through a variety of methods, most of them fairly traditional. We read textbooks and saw videos. I gave short lectures and my students took notes. We worked on vocabulary, maps, and timelines, usually spending two or three weeks building a general background for a particular period of history. Then, as a culminating project, we'd do one of these very inten-sive Complex Instruction investigations. These were always centered on a major concept significant to a specific era we were studying and had broader, even contemporary, connections as well. In one case it was How Do Historians Know About the Crusades? The primary sources used visuals, music, and graphics to investigate, and the tempting projects included rap songs, models, skits, and murals.

As we alternated between whole-class direct instruc-tion, individual seatwork, pairs, and groups, my students became very proficient at moving their desks and reconfiguring the room with a minimum of fuss. They worked in groups for some kind of activity nearly every day, sometimes for reading discussion or writing groups, at other times for social studies investigations or reviews. Sometimes I carefully composed each group. Occasionally I allowed students to form their own. Most of the time I assigned groups randomly, changing them with each unit and rotating the roles with each activity. As the students gained confidence in the process and accepted more of the responsibility, the quality of their work steadily improved.

I was happy with this progress, but as I saw students assuming new roles in their own learning processes, I also saw my own role changing. I no longer felt I was at the center of this steadily revolving wheel.

For the third unit, Christi and Roberto ended up in the same group again, and one day their lively discussion caught my attention. They were trying to design an ad campaign for the Children's Crusade and struggling with the constraints of an illiterate populace. Roberto had some very strong opinions about what would work for people who couldn't read the poster; he became very animated about using color and drawings, not just as decoration, but to convey meaning. Christi and Maria thought drawings would be too hard to figure out; they wanted more written explanation. For his part, Kevin was trying hard to satisfy everybody.

After some discussion, Christi became agitated and was clearly fighting hard to control herself. Maria explained why she and Christi were upset. "We had it all planned out and now they want to go and mess it up with all this other stuff," she said. Christi seemed to calm down when Kevin suggested several possible compromises.

As I moved away, Roberto caught my eye and said, "Before, my group complained when I didn't talk, and now they complain when I do." But his mouth and eyes were smiling as he turned quickly back to his group to press his point one more time.

Theirs was a healthy debate, and I could see that their differences were leading them into a critical discussion. So I left them to work it out for themselves.

Of course, problems still arose, and many times they centered on Christi. No matter who else was in a group, things rarely went smoothly with her in it.

I had a lot of contact with her outside the core class. She was in the leadership class and student government, both of which I advised. At this time she happened to be in charge of decorating for the Valentine's Day Dance. In preparation for the dance, committees had been making what seemed to be thousands of hearts in all sizes. At 3 p.m., 25 to 30 kids began stringing hearts around the multipurpose room, ostensibly under Christi's command. I was called upon repeatedly to settle artistic disputes. At 3:30, individuals began to drift away, and by 4:30, only a handful of girls remained working. But there was Christi, up on a ladder, working her way around the room, creating a fantastic mural of pink, red, and white hearts. She finally finished at 6:45, and it was beautiful. At 7 p.m. we opened the doors and the dance began.

The praise was lavish and genuine. Christi took it graciously, saying, "Everybody helped. I just finished putting them up."

On the way home I thought a lot about committees and groupwork, about individuals and initiative. I thought a lot about Christi's problems with groupwork, and I thought a lot about my own.

As the class increasingly internalized the group process, Christi's problems became more extreme. The less I was needed elsewhere, the more time I spent rescuing whichever group she happened to be in. Often we spent more time on conflict management strategies than on the curriculum. Sometimes the situation was explosive. Christi would shout, stomp her foot, sulk, and cry. I was less and less able to reason with her, and increasingly I began to remove her from the group. I would make her take a time-out in the hall or sit at a desk away from the group until she was willing to go back and make peace. Then the group had to be willing to have her back. They always said yes and were usually gracious about it. Christi was usually able to work harmoniously once she returned.

Some other students frequently had problems, too—Eddy, for example. One of the most popular boys in school, he was cute, athletic, and physically mature. But academically he was insecure and anxious, usually doing just enough to pass and often announcing that he could have gotten better grades if he'd wanted to. Eddy hated groupwork, and as with Christi's groups, his frequently erupted in argument, accusation, and blame. I couldn't find the key to helping him feel more confident. Eventually, other students became reluctant to have either Christi or Eddy in their groups.

Eric's situation was a little different. Passive and withdrawn, he generally avoided everyone except his one friend, Jimmy. It took me a long while to realize that Eric was quite bright. Once I did, I began to try to create more opportunities within his groups for him to use his abilities. I was determined that what had worked with Roberto would also work with Eric. I stepped in whenever I saw an opportunity to praise his contributions, telling the rest of the group to listen to Eric. He seemed to make progress. Whenever he caught me watching him he became an animated participant in his group, usually making some significant contribution. Convinced that he was getting hooked, I continued to praise him. I often put Jimmy in his group to lend encouragement and support.

Then one day, when I acknowledged something Eric had said that was pertinent to the task, Tran Pham, a girl who worked well with everyone, spoke up in exasperation.

"Ms. Knight," she said, "he sits there and knows things but he'll never help us or tell us until you come along. He won't say anything until he sees you watching or you come over here—even when we ask him and ask him!"

Initially I felt betrayed, and I resolved to leave Eric to the mercies of the group. I was both angry and confused, again questioning what my role here was supposed to be. Sometimes it felt as if the class had moved on and left me behind.

There were less obvious successes and failures, too.

Desiree, a large, quiet girl who was often absent, had always seemed self-conscious and shy, so it was a real surprise to everyone when she performed so well in her group's skit. Though her body remained stiff and wooden, her voice and facial expressions made the show. She dismissed her success by saying that she didn't like to do it but had to for the group. But people started wanting her in their group, asking her opinion about skits and about other things, too. Though Desiree still had a lot of absences, she always came to school when she knew we were doing groupwork.

Leo had quite a reputation as a tough kid in school, one who had even beaten up some eighth graders. A few kids in class feared him, while others courted his protection. I knew Leo's family was from Samoa and suspected that he had some language difficulties. Although he never made trouble in class, he did not pay attention or know what was going on. He maintained an air of indifference, never turning in any work. Although we all knew he could draw, no one suspected that Leo was also musical. After that first poetry project with the rap, it became apparent that Leo could make an instrument out of almost anything and easily put a beat to any words someone else might write. Working in the group, he seemed to understand more of the subtleties of language in the songs and poems, and he helped others understand the rhythm and pattern. With Leo's small successes, his tough facade started to fade and he began to show interest in other aspects of classwork.

Cyndi was failing in all her classes. Her home life was a mess and was mirrored in her disorganized binder and her confused and scattered responses to everything. She never seemed to know which class she was in or what she was supposed to be doing there, but she had an incredible eye for visual detail. During her group projects, she made very precise observations and added the touches that finished things off just perfectly. The class continued to regard Cyndi as more than a little

weird, but they listened to what she had to say and carefully considered her suggestions. In turn, she made a real effort to tune in to what was going on. At the end-of-the-year social studies test, the only questions she answered were those on material covered through groupwork.

None of these kids became A+ students. There were no overnight successes, no instant turn-arounds, no sudden stars. But among this handful of students for whom academic success had been so elusive, I witnessed small increments of increased interest and involvement. In spite of the problems groupwork highlighted for some students and the questions it raised for me about my role, I became convinced that groupwork had to become a central part of my classroom rather than a peripheral activity.

When it came time to study medieval Japan, Christi, Eddy, and Roberto were teamed up again. The activities required each group to investigate some aspect of social stratification in medieval Japanese society. This particular group was to design and build a Japanese castle town, showing the ways in which even the design of the castle and the layout of the town reflected considerations of rank and power.

Eddy immediately took command and Christi eagerly became second lieutenant, completely excluding Roberto. He wasn't even allowed to pick up the materials. Eddy did the building and grunted out orders: "Where's the tape? Get me something to put here. Find the scissors." Christi fetched whatever he called for and then stood silently beside him, handing him whatever was needed. There was no discussion, no investigation—just single-minded concentration on completing the product as quickly and painlessly as possible. Roberto tried to make some valuable suggestions about some of the castle details but was ignored. Their castle ended up looking more European than Japanese, and they had done nothing about the surrounding town. In the end, I noted that some of the missing details were ones Roberto had tried to suggest. I said discussion might have resulted in their inclusion of more of those possibilities.

Eddy was outraged, crying, "You never like anything I do!"

Christi just seemed sad and resigned.

A few weeks later a similar situation arose: Jonathan and Christi got into a terrible argument that included tears and tantrums. But by now so many others in the class had begun to enjoy the group activities that it was clear to me Christi was way out of line. I removed her for a time-out, making no attempt to mediate, and I began to wonder if I had not been contributing to her problem by giving it so much attention. Maybe my interventions had only fueled the situation, reinforcing both Christi's and my need to be at center stage, to be in charge.

It was a startling and painful consideration, made more so by what was going on in another group. I was aware that LaToya, Jimmy, Desiree, and Leo had been very busy bustling about the room, collecting additional resource books, looking, discussing, arguing productively, pointing things out, and working on their poster. I couldn't figure out what exactly was going on, but I could tell that some small dispute had at least temporarily stalled their progress. I couldn't resist intruding.

"Is there a problem?" I asked.

"Oh, no. We're okay, Ms. Knight," said one member. The rest barely paused to acknowledge me.

But I couldn't leave it alone. Opened in front of them were a couple of different dictionaries, a thesaurus, and several encyclopedias. Curious, I asked what they were looking for.

LaToya paused for a moment as the others continued. "We're trying to find out for sure what a Papal bull is," she said. "We think we know but want to be sure."

"We've found papal and pope and bull but not Papal bull," Jimmy added. "We're trying to put it together so it makes sense."

"That's a pretty difficult and specialized term," I commented. Then, almost plaintively, I said, "Why didn't you just ask me?"

With more understanding and sense than I had exhibited, LaToya replied, "Because we knew you'd just tell us that together we were smart enough to figure it out for ourselves."

On the very last day of groupwork, about two weeks before the end of school, I had to remove Christi from her group for the final time. They had been preparing a skit and she was being extremely obstinate. I had her sit on a chair near my desk. Sometime later, when she said she was ready to go back to her group, I said, "No, Christi. Sometimes you just can't go back and pick up where you left off. Your group has gone on without you and they are ready to present to the class. This time, all you can do is watch."

I know she understood. But tears filled her eyes and she put her head down on the desk and silently sobbed. A little while later, when her group did their presentation, her whole body showed how she longed to be part of their fun, yet she joined the rest of the class in enthusiastic applause. There were still tears in her eyes, and as I watched her, there were tears in mine, too. I felt both exhilarated and sad. Whatever had happened to Christi had happened to me as well.

ANNOTATED BIBLIOGRAPHY ON GROUPWORK

GENERAL INFORMATION AND RESOURCES

Brandt, Ronald (Ed.). (1991). *Readings from educational leadership: Cooperative learning and the collaborative school.* Alexandria, VA: The Association for Supervision and Curriculum Development (ASCD).

> This volume is a collection of articles on cooperative learning and collaborative schools drawn from *Educational Leadership* between 1987 and 1991. The articles are practical and easy to read and provide an excellent opportunity for newcomers and skilled groupwork practitioners both to familiarize and to deepen their understanding of cooperative learning concepts, research, and strategies. Included are general introductions to groupwork, descriptions of specific methods, suggestions for implementing activities, recommendations for staff development, documentation of research findings, discussion of controversial issues in the field, and strategies for designing collaborative school environments. Readers with practical interests will appreciate the numerous case studies and lesson plans illustrating cooperative planning and groupwork in action. *Note:* Those who subscribe to *Educational Leadership* may wish to refer directly to back issues on cooperative learning (volume 47, number 4) and collegial support (volume 45, number 3).

Sharan, Shlomo (Ed.). (1994). *Handbook of cooperative learning methods.* Westport, CT: Green Press.

> This book presents a broad, thorough overview of cooperative learning, providing descriptions of groupwork methods and applications as well as insights on implementation. Contributing authors include leaders in the cooperative learning field such as Robert Slavin, David and Roger Johnson, Elizabeth Cohen, Yael and Shlomo Sharan, Spencer Kagan, and Neil Davidson.
>
> The first eight chapters describe the most well-known and researched models of cooperative learning—Student Teams–Achievement Divisions (STAD), Team Assisted Individualization (TAI), Cooperative Integrated Reading and Composition (CIRC), Jigsaw, Learning Together, Structured Academic Controversy, Complex Instruction, Group Investigation, and Kagan's Structural Approach. Chapters 9–16 describe the application of a number of generic models of groupwork to specific academic disciplines, including literature and language arts, language development, science, mathematics, and computers. Also considered is the contribution of cooperative learning to psychological, cognitive, and metacognitive development and functioning in learning.
>
> Sharan concludes with several chapters on the challenges of long-term implementation of cooperative learning. The need for building a sense of community within the school, expanding staff development, fostering collaborative planning and collegial coaching, and creating congruence between the social organization of the classroom and the school are discussed. These chapters suggest there are a number of factors that must be considered carefully if cooperative learning is to be implemented successfully and maintained on a wide-scale, long-term basis.

International Association for the Study of Cooperation in Education. *Cooperative Learning.*

> This quarterly magazine, published by the International Association for the Study of Cooperation in Education (IASCE), provides practical, easy-to-read information and strategies to educators interested in improving instructional effectiveness and learning through cooperative groupwork. Quarterly issues are generally thematic in nature and include articles by leaders in the field, interviews with experienced groupwork practitioners, current research findings, lesson plans and tips from classroom teachers, suggestions for staff development, ideas for combining computers and cooperative learning, reviews of books and videos, and a calendar of upcoming events and training.
>
> At least fourteen back issues can currently be ordered. Thematic topics include science, mathematics, language arts, social studies, critical thinking, assessment, staff development, higher education, and school community.

IASCE also publishes a resource guide describing additional cooperative learning resources.

Cooperative Learning is a benefit for members of IASCE. For membership information and details on ordering back issues, readers may write to IASCE—*Cooperative Learning* at Box 1582, Santa Cruz, CA 95061-1582, or call (408) 426-7926.

MODELS OF COOPERATIVE LEARNING

Aronson, Elliott, et al. (1978). *The jigsaw classroom.* Beverly Hills, CA: Sage.

Aronson describes the origins and procedural details of jigsaw, a cooperative learning method that makes use of reconstituted work groups in the classroom. This approach to cooperative learning involves dividing an academic lesson among members of a heterogeneous home group. Each home group member joins an expert group to master materials associated with a specific dimension of the lesson's topic. Students then return to their home groups to teach teammates what they have learned. A benefit of this model is the positive interdependence created when students are required to specialize in subject matter and present it to others.

Aronson complements his description of jigsaw and its history with sample curriculum and classroom activities. In addition, he provides suggestions for implementation, emphasizing the need to build cooperative social skills, transform the teacher's role to one of facilitator, and develop group leadership within each cooperative learning team.

Though this book is now out of print, it can be obtained in a number of university libraries. Summaries of Aronson's jigsaw model also appear in several texts, including Shlomo Sharan's *Handbook of Cooperative Learning Methods* and Spencer Kagan's *Cooperative Learning: Resources for Teachers.*

Cohen, Elizabeth G., & Lotan, Rachel A. (Eds.). (1997). *Working for equity in heterogeneous classrooms: Sociological theory in practice.* New York: Teachers College Press.

In this volume, Cohen, Lotan, and other authors present the theoretical framework and empirical findings for Complex Instruction, an approach to teaching at a high level in academically heterogeneous classrooms. When a teacher delegates authority, students serve as resources to one another as they work on challenging, open-ended group tasks that require the use of multiple abilities. Teachers pay particular attention to creating equal-status interaction in the small working groups. Studies of Complex Instruction classrooms at the elementary and middle school levels have documented gains on standardized achievement and content-referenced tests, and on measures of cognitive development and English language proficiency.

With a strong basis in theory, the authors have carefully studied aspects of the implementation of Complex Instruction in classrooms with ethnically, linguistically, and academically mixed student populations. They have related the quality of implementation to the organizational conditions at the school and to the professional interactions with staff developers.

Cohen, Elizabeth G. (1994). *Designing groupwork: Strategies for the heterogeneous classroom* (2nd ed.). New York: Teachers College Press.

Cohen provides an excellent introduction to cooperative learning in the heterogeneous classroom. She begins by offering a general definition of groupwork and a rationale for including cooperative groupwork in one's instructional repertoire. Cohen cites research documenting the effectiveness of cooperative learning—specifically, the benefits of student–student interaction in learning. She describes practical strategies for preparing students for groupwork, how to plan cooperative tasks, how to evaluate cooperative learning experiences, and the role of the teacher in a cooperative classroom. Throughout the text are classroom scenarios and group activities illustrating key concepts. The appendixes include practical evaluation tools and cooperative training exercises to prepare students for successful groupwork.

Throughout *Designing Groupwork,* Cohen focuses on three features central to successful cooperative learning experiences: delegating authority to students, creating positive interdependence, and promoting student-to-student interaction. In addition, she stresses the importance of treating status problems that commonly result in unequal participation and undesirable domination of learning groups by high-status students. To combat this problem, Cohen introduces two treatments that, when used in combination, can equalize participation and alter expectations for competence of low status students during cooperative group activities.

Johnson, David W., & Johnson, Roger T. (1994). *Learning together and alone: Cooperative, competitive, and individualistic learning* (4th ed.). Englewood Cliffs, NJ: Prentice Hall.

David and Roger Johnson discuss Learning Together, a conceptual model of cooperative learning that encompasses the entire school community. The Johnsons' intent is to help educators create a collaborative school environment and combine cooperative, competitive, and individualistic learning into an overall instructional framework. They advocate the use of three effectively structured groupwork strategies (formal, informal, and base groups), development of "appropriate" competitive and individualistic learning activities, establishment of cooperative classroom routines, and a shift in the organization of the school from a mass-production structure to a cooperative team-based structure.

The Johnsons explain how to structure an effective cooperative lesson, carefully defining and explaining five components they believe essential to successful cooperative learning experiences—positive interdependence, face-to-face interaction, individual accountability, social skills, and group processing. In addition, they provide practical guidelines for creating constructive learning activities, both competitive and individualistic. Also included is information on utilizing structured academic controversy, developing social skills, teaching conflict resolution, assessing groupwork experiences, and creating opportunities to reflect on learning, and tips for dealing with at-risk and gifted students in cooperative learning environments.

Kagan, Spencer. (1992). *Cooperative learning: Resources for teachers* (2nd ed.). San Juan Capistrano, CA: Resources for Teachers.

Kagan provides an outline of his structural approach to cooperative learning, including an introduction to general cooperative theory and research; descriptions of numerous content-free procedures for encouraging groupwork; and practical charts, lesson designs, and reproducible handouts to make cooperative learning effective. Kagan's approach to groupwork centers on "structures," which he defines as ways of organizing interaction among individuals in the classroom. Structures relate to the "how" of instruction and can be combined flexibly with any subject matter to form infinite cooperative learning activities. He organizes instructional structures into six categories based on the learning objectives they best promote. These objectives are team building, class building, communication building, information exchange, mastery, and thinking skills. In addition, he offers methods for forming learning teams and useful strategies for managing the cooperative classroom.

The final chapters describe several complex lesson designs for mastery, task specialization, and group projects and provide suggestions for developing a cooperative school environment. The book concludes with a list of cooperative learning resources.

Sharan, Shlomo, & Sharan, Yael. (1992). *Expanding cooperative learning through group investigation*. New York: Teachers College Press.

Yael and Shlomo Sharan explain Group Investigation, a cooperative learning strategy that combines student-student interaction and academic inquiry. The student is central to this groupwork model, taking an active part in selecting topics of study, establishing learning goals, planning and implementing tasks, presenting projects to the class, evaluating completed work, and reflecting on investigative learning experiences.

The Sharans preface their description of Group Investigation with a discussion of the theory underlying their method and an empirically sound argument for using group-structured academic inquiry in the classroom. They stress the importance of setting the stage for complex group inquiry by preparing students to work together in groups, to help each other, and to share materials, information, and ideas. Specifically, they recommend teachers purposely develop their students' discussion skills, cooperative planning abilities, and other social skills by utilizing skillbuilding exercises, cooperative norms, behavior modeling, legitimization of interaction as a route to learning, and reflection time following learning experiences.

The Sharans outline six consecutive stages of group investigation, describing the steps involved in implementing them and articulating both teacher and student roles at each level. The authors keep the practitioner in mind, offering numerous skillbuilding exercises and lesson plans. An entire chapter is devoted to describing interesting and inspiring real-life group investigation projects in a variety of subjects at several grade levels.

Slavin, Robert E. (1991). *Student team learning* (2nd ed.). Washington DC: National Education Association.

Slavin introduces several models of Student Team Learning—cooperative learning strategies involving a combination of direct instruction via teacher or text, team study, individual assessment, and team recognition. Slavin first provides detailed instructions for implementing Student Teams Achievement Divisions (STAD) and Teams-Games-Tournaments (TGT), two methods of cooperative learning that are appropriate for teaching basic skills with clearly defined objectives and single correct answers. Both methods may be used at any grade level with any subject, using teacher-generated materials or curricula developed by Slavin and his colleagues at Johns Hopkins. Next Slavin outlines the procedural steps of jigsaw II, his version of Aronson's original jigsaw method. Finally, he describes Teams Accelerated Instruction (TAI) and Cooperative Integrated Reading and Composition (CIRC). Unlike STAD, TGT, and jigsaw II, these models are content bound in math and language arts, respectively, and require special curriculum materials prepared at Johns Hopkins.

In addition to providing procedural information, Slavin explains the three primary concepts of his student team approach to cooperative learning—team rewards, individual accountability, and equal opportunities for success. He also includes a section on troubleshooting common problems, including conflicts among group members, general misbehavior, excessive noise, absenteeism, and ineffective use of team study time.

COOPERATIVE LEARNING IN THE DISCIPLINES

MATHEMATICS

Davidson, Neil (Ed.). (1990). *Cooperative learning in mathematics: A handbook for teachers*. Reading, MA: Addison-Wesley.

This text presents strategies for incorporating cooperative groupwork into mathematics instruction and learning. Most of the strategies can be used at the elementary, secondary, and post-secondary levels and include methods appropriate both for mastering basic math facts and developing problem solving and mathematical reasoning abilities. Contributing authors present ideas and methods for structuring math-related cooperative groupwork, preparing students for cooperative math learning, managing the classroom, designing appropriate group tasks, and troubleshooting problems associated with cooperative learning. Specific methods discussed include Groups of Four, Complex Instruction (Finding Out/*Descubrimiento*), Learning Together, Real Maths, STAD, TGT, TAI, jigsaw II, Small Group Lab Approach, and Small Group Discovery Method.

A common theme is evident in the models compiled by Davidson. Whether implicitly or explicitly, most authors suggest cooperative groupwork can facilitate achievement of the recently reformed goals of mathematics instruction. The contributors imply that math teaching and learning should move from rote memorization of technical symbols and mastery of computational skills toward math concepts, the development of problem solving competency, mathematical reasoning, and the ability to communicate mathematically. Additionally they recommended that teachers help students to value math and build "math confidence" in them by presenting the subject in meaningful real-life contexts, highlighting the connections between mathematics and other disciplines, and demonstrating that all students can learn math.

Throughout the text, cooperative groupwork is advocated as an instructional method congruent with these evolving goals. The contributing authors suggest that verbalizing and discussing mathematical thought processes during groupwork and being exposed to the thinking of others helps students clarify, develop, and expand their mathematical thinking over time. Among the expected results are enhanced academic performance and increased math-related esteem.

SOCIAL STUDIES

Stahl, Robert J. (Ed.). (1994). *Cooperative learning in social studies: A handbook for teachers*. New York: Addison-Wesley.

This collection of essays offers techniques for using cooperative learning within social studies classrooms. Robert Stahl introduces the book with an overview of cooperative learning, including a description of its central elements and an argument why groupwork is compatible with the achievement of highly valued social studies outcomes—human dignity, rational thinking, humane and civil behavior, and active and responsible citizenship. Stahl's introduction is followed by a chapter outlining generic tips for preparing for groupwork and managing it. Suggestions are provided for cultivating cooperative skills, forming learning teams, addressing status issues, and monitoring the natural stages of group development.

The core of the book is specific groupwork strategies for social studies. Seven common and well-researched models of cooperative learning are described—Learning Together, jigsaw, STAD, TGT, Group Investigation, Co-op Co-op, and Kagan's structural approach. Several other methods are introduced, including a pro-con cooperative strategy, individual-group decision making episodes, and a group approach to traditional social studies research papers and reports. All chapters are practical, emphasizing the "how-to" of the techniques described. Many examples and scenarios, as well as cooperative checklists, forms, and tables, are provided to help guide teachers to successfully use the strategies presented.

SCIENCE

International Association for the Study of Cooperation in Education. (1991, April). "Cooperative learning and science." *Cooperative Learning, 11*(3).

This issue of *Cooperative Learning* explores how collaborative groupwork can improve learning in science classrooms. Contributing authors promote a hands-on approach to science in which students together engage in experiential processes of science inquiry. Descriptions of five of the methods follow.

"Teaming Up" is a six-step process of skill-based science inquiry involving group investigation. "Life Lab Curriculum" employs a cooperative approach to science involving indoor and outdoor gardens and community involvement. "Cheche Konnen" is designed especially for language minority students and utilizes a collaborative interdisciplinary approach to science. Students act as scientists, posing science questions and designing and implementing research projects to explore their questions. "Finding Out/*Descubrimiento*" consists of an interactive, hands-on math and science curriculum that promotes conceptual learning and builds thinking skills for elementary school students. The curriculum is bilingual and utilizes the Complex Instruction approach to groupwork developed by Dr. Elizabeth Cohen. "Project AIMS [Activities for Integrating Math and Science]" integrates science and math learning through cooperative activities consisting of real world experiences, oral and written communication, pictorial and graphic communication, and critical thinking.

Two articles address computer-based cooperative learning in science. Both authors suggest that computers can enhance groupwork and describe ways to utilize computers in the classroom (i.e., word processing for group writing, and databases to support cooperative inquiry). Mary Male discusses several software programs that promote group problem solving and mastery of science concepts and skills. Among the programs suggested are several produced by Sunburst and Wings for Learning, including *Learn About Animals*, *Learn About Plants*, *Learn About Insects*, *Animal Trackers*, *Exploring Tidepools*, *Voyage of the Mimi*, and *Playing with Science: Motion*.

Finally, experts reviewed several books that are of value to science teachers interested in incorporating cooperative learning into their instructional repertoires—*The Growing Classroom: Garden-Based Science*, *Science Experiences: Cooperative Learning*, *Teaching of Science*, and *Teaming Up*.

LITERATURE AND LANGUAGE ARTS

International Association for the Study of Cooperation in Education. (1991, July). "Co-op learning and language arts: Learning to communicate—communicating to learn." *Cooperative Learning*, 11(4).

> This thematic issue of *Cooperative Learning* provides insight into how groupwork can be used to teach reading, writing, and other language arts concepts and skills. Most articles are written by classroom teachers and describe specific models of cooperative learning applied to language arts. Patrick Dias, for example, introduces an approach to teaching poetry through small group discussion. In this method, students work together to read and find meaning in poems with a minimum of interpretive support from the teacher. Marjorie Beggs discusses "Children's Own Stories," a method that encourages students to tell about their lives: they dictate personal real or made-up stories to the teacher or a trained volunteer who records them verbatim. Stories are then shared and illustrated within cooperative groups. This particular approach helps language minority students develop their fluency by verbalizing and reading personally familiar stories. Robert Slavin outlines a cooperative-based reading and language arts curriculum involving basal reading activities, direct instruction in reading comprehension, independent reading, and integrated language arts and writing. In this program, called Cooperative Integrated Reading and Composition (CIRC), students work with partners and in groups on activities including partner reading, spelling, story retelling, group writing, and reading comprehension. Other models presented include a cooperative

learning and literature planning model, partner exchange journals, and writing clubs.

> An article by Mary Male describes how to design and plan computer-based cooperative language arts activities. She outlines a step-by-step procedure for cooperative writing and suggests how to select word processing programs for group writing, schedule sequences of on- and off-computer activities, and choose literature to use to stimulate writing. In addition, Male recommends several software programs and publications to support the development of cooperative whole language curricula.

> The issue ends with book reviews relevant to cooperative learning and language arts. Among works reviewed are *Perspectives on Small Group Learning: Theory and Practice*; *Focus on Collaborative Learning: Classroom Practices in Teaching English*; *Literature and Cooperative Learning*; *The English Workshop Series*; *A Part to Play: Tips, Techniques, and Tools for Learning Cooperatively*; and *Celebrate Units: A Guide for Incorporating Whole Language and Cooperate Learning for All Classrooms*. Also included is a bibliography on whole language resources.

LANGUAGE DEVELOPMENT

Kessler, Carolyn (Ed.). (1992). *Cooperative language learning: A teacher's resource book*. Englewood Cliffs, NJ: Prentice Hall.

> This compilation of essays addresses the application of cooperative methods to second language instruction and learning. While the emphasis is on teaching students with limited English proficiency, the concepts and strategies presented are equally applicable to the teaching of foreign languages.

> The first section, "Foundations of Cooperative Learning," explains the process of cooperative learning and explores the beneficial effect of groupwork on overall academic achievement and language acquisition. Key elements of effective groupwork are described, including positive interdependence, individual accountability, social skill development, heterogeneous team formation, team building, and group size. In addition, several models of

cooperative learning are introduced—Learning Together, Spencer Kagan's structural approach, and specific cooperative curriculum packages (i.e., Finding Out/ *Descubrimiento* and CIRC). Throughout these chapters authors advocate a communicative approach to language development and suggest that cooperative learning supports such an approach because of the opportunities to engage in authentic communication. Through cooperative interaction and thought, students learn verbal expression, as well as content-related concepts and skills.

Chapters 4–7, "Language and Content," examine cooperative learning in content-based language instruction. The focus is on how teachers can help students with limited English proficiency develop simultaneously language skills and subject matter knowledge in science, social studies, and math. In addition, the jigsaw model of cooperative learning is introduced and promoted as a useful instructional strategy for integrating language and content.

The final four chapters focus on teachers in cooperative learning environments. Key elements of the teacher's role before, during, and after groupwork are described. Teacher talk in traditional and cooperative settings is compared, and the latter is shown to better support the communicative approach to language development. One chapter promotes the incorporation of cooperative learning into graduate programs for ESL and foreign language teachers. It is recommended that individuals in such programs learn *about* cooperative groupwork *via* groupwork in preparation for using this strategy in their classrooms. Strategies for designing and implementing staff development programs to help existing teachers build competence in using cooperative learning are also provided.

The volume concludes with a bibliography that includes general resources on cooperative learning, ESL literature, and additional topics.

COMPUTERS

Male, Mary. (1994). "Cooperative learning and computers." In Shlomo Sharan (Ed.), *Handbook of cooperative learning methods*. Westport, CT: Green Press.

In this brief article, Male challenges teachers to put computers to powerful use in their classrooms. Specifically, she encourages them to utilize computers to engage students in rich, collaborative learning experiences, rather than traditional drill and practice exercises. To support this suggestion, Male recommends educational software packages that encourage cooperative learning and discusses essentials teachers should include when designing computer-based groupwork—heterogeneous groups, team building, social skills development, positive interdependence, individual accountability, and group processing. In addition, she describes four ways computers can be used within the classroom (group writing/ word processing, problem solving, database generation and use, and academic review), providing a sample lesson plan for each.

COOPERATIVE LEARNING AND CRITICAL THINKING

Davidson, Neil, & Worsham, Tony (Eds.). (1992). *Enhancing thinking through cooperative learning*. New York: Teachers College Press.

The essays in this book connect two important trends in education: thinking improvement and cooperative learning. Contributing authors stress thought and metacognition in the overall learning process, and specifically, the importance of creating a genuine understanding of subject content. Cooperative learning is advocated as an effective approach for developing and reinforcing students' capacity to think and reflect individually and in groups. The book explains the beneficial effects of cooperative thought and interaction and offers practical information on how to build thinking skills through collaboration. Phases of learning, as well as indicators of intelligent behavior, are discussed, and suggestions for using groupwork to enhance thinking at all levels are provided. Several practical strategies and tools for cooperative thought are described in detail, including group discussion methods, cooperative-based graphic organizers, and question generation techniques.

Several authors extend their thoughts beyond the classroom, suggesting that teaching cooperative thought in school is necessary to meet the need for cooperative problem solving in the workplace and within society in general.

COOPERATIVE LEARNING AND SOCIAL SKILLS

Johnson, David W., & Johnson, F. P. (1994). *Joining together: Group theory and group skills* (5th ed.). Englewood Cliffs, NJ: Prentice-Hall.

This book blends group theory and practical skillbuilding exercises to help readers develop the cooperative competencies necessary for effective groupwork. The Johnsons' premise is that simply placing individuals on teams will not ensure successful group experiences; cooperative skills need to be taught and learned directly. *Joining Together* is a tool to facilitate this process. Teachers can use the text to gain insight on working collaboratively with peers and preparing students for cooperative learning.

Chapters 1 and 2 present a theoretical overview of group dynamics and experiential learning and lay a foundation for the remaining chapters covering ten cooperative skill areas: group goals and social interdependence, communication, leadership, decision making, academic controversy and creativity, conflict resolution, the use of power, dealing with diversity, leading discussion and counseling groups, and team building. Each chapter covers relevant theory and research and includes diagnostic and practice exercises and simulations designed to help readers develop and refine specific cooperative social skills.

COOPERATIVE LEARNING ASSESSMENT

International Association for the Study of Cooperation in Education. (1992, Fall). "Assessment in cooperative learning." *Cooperative Learning, 13*(1).

This issue focuses on assessment and evaluation in cooperative learning settings. Several general themes emerge. First, there is consensus that the assessment and evaluation process should consider, at minimum, knowledge and skills acquired, as well as students' ability to work with others and respond effectively to problem situations. Authors suggest a variety of methods for assessing student academic and social progress, including ongoing teacher monitoring and feedback, self-evaluation, peer evaluation, individual and group reflection and processing, exams, and a host of individual

and group products, including essays, books, videos, slide presentations, museum-like displays, skits, role-plays, and oral reports. Most authors agree that students should be involved in establishing evaluation criteria and in evaluating their own and their peers' work. However, they suggest that such involvement take place only after students are familiar with the process of cooperative learning and the concept of evaluation.

In addition to assessment methods, the authors comment on appropriate tasks for evaluating student behavior and quality of learning in cooperative groups. A primary concern is the need to provide all students with a fair chance to interact with teammates and demonstrate what they learn. To facilitate this, authors suggest that groupwork tasks be structured to encourage interdependence, have clearly defined learning outcomes, accommodate a variety of learning styles, allow students to reveal conceptual understanding and new skills in varied ways, and include status treatments to equalize interaction between high- and low-status students.

Two articles address the usefulness of cooperative learning in assessing the academic and affective development of students with limited English proficiency. Both authors assert that traditional methods of assessment (e.g., standardized tests) do not provide teachers with adequate information to determine knowledge gains or learning needs of ESL students, therefore hindering the customization of instruction for this group. Cooperative learning offers one potential solution to this assessment challenge. Because groupwork provides opportunities for student–student interaction and encourages verbalization of thinking, it can give teachers a view into students' minds as they construct knowledge. By observing students during cooperative activities, teachers can see how students use what they know, what students do or do not understand about concepts being studied, and students' levels of literacy and fluency in their first and second languages. Two models of cooperative learning designed specifically for bilingual students are described: Finding Out/*Descubrimiento* (math and science), and CIRC (English and language arts).

Other topics of discussion include the use of computers in assessment and evaluation, authentic assessment in the cooperative classroom, development of self-monitoring cards to assist students in practicing and internalizing helping behaviors, and student assessment criteria for a range of evaluation procedures (traditional to radical).

COOPERATIVE LEARNING AND STAFF DEVELOPMENT

International Association for the Study of Cooperation in Education. (1991–1992, Winter). "Staff development: Building communities of learners." *Cooperative Learning, 12*(2).

This issue focuses on the need to reengineer staff development programs on cooperative learning. The call for "new and improved" training programs stems from the belief that many teachers don't use cooperative learning to its fullest potential due to a lack of adequate training and support. The articles herein describe effective cooperative learning training, as well as successful staff development strategies and programs related to cooperative groupwork. Contributors suggest that cooperative learning training must be ongoing, help teachers understand the theoretical concepts of group-based learning, *and* build competence in designing and implementing specific cooperative strategies. Moreover, they recommend that training interventions be experiential in nature, providing demonstrations of cooperative learning strategies and giving teachers opportunities to practice groupwork in the workshop setting. Two articles offer tips to staff developers for creating and leading workshops and institutes that will capture and hold teachers' attention.

Contributors also assert that quality cooperative learning workshops and institutes alone will not guarantee effective and sustained use of groupwork. Training, they say, must continue at the school site and involve ongoing practice, evaluation, and reflection. They suggest teachers be encouraged to use cooperative learning in their classrooms and be given access to networks of support, regular evaluation, and coaching from peers, staff developers, and administrators. Collaborative lesson planning and reflection are also highly recommended.

Several articles describe successful staff development strategies and tools that teachers and schools can incorporate into their cooperative learning training programs. One such tool is a chart that outlines levels of competence in implementing and using cooperative learning. Teachers can use this "innovation profile" to determine beginning, intermediate, and advanced levels of the practice of cooperative learning. Then they can assess their current levels of competence and set personal goals. Another strategy, termed "teachers as researchers," involves a team approach to reading cooperative learning literature, reflecting on personal experiences, and accumulating and analyzing data related to outcomes of cooperative learning in the classroom. Other strategies and tools described address principles of teamwork, key characteristics of leadership, and ideas for teaching groupwork as an instructional practice to preservice teachers.

Guidelines for Writing Cases

This casebook provides a way of capturing veteran teachers' knowledge about groupwork in diverse classrooms. Though small group instruction has been practiced and studied for more than twenty years, research literature has seldom addressed the craft knowledge teachers acquire through the messiness of classroom life. The cases in this book illustrate the dilemmas and challenges teachers face when using groupwork.

WHAT DO WE MEAN BY A CASE?

A case is not merely a narrative or description of any particular event or series of events. Rather, we make a theoretical claim that it is a "case of something." For this book, contributors can select from nine possible topics, such as "complexities of teaching" or "delegating authority" (see below). Each case tells a story. It describes what led up to an event and the consequences that followed. To the extent possible, it also describes how the participants in the event were thinking and feeling.

WRITING A CASE

A compelling case for this volume should be built around a problem, a challenge, or a dilemma that can be common to many teachers. It's best to select a problem for which your first attempt to deal with it didn't work. You tried to resolve it with several alternatives before succeeding or giving up. Try to think of a situation where questions can be raised about how best to approach a problem.

The most compelling cases are written with some dramatic quality. The problems are written so that readers will identify immediately with the teacher who confronts the problem and will want to know what happened. Don't worry about the quality of your writing in the first draft. You will have opportunities to revise and polish. Editing will also be done before a case is published.

Structure of a case. First, describe your problem, identifying who you are. Next, provide some context (type of school, students, community). Then write as vivid an account as you can. Specifically indicate if/when the cultural or ethnic background of students (and language) played an important part in your teaching intervention or practice. When appropriate, end your case with some unresolved questions.

In a second section, briefly reflect on your narrative. If a similar situation were to occur again, would you do anything differently? Why?

TOPICS TO CONSIDER

The proposed organizational framework for *Groupwork in Diverse Classrooms: A Casebook for Educators* is represented below. Please select one topic for your case.

Curriculum and Instruction

1. Developing appropriate curriculum. One of the biggest challenges in making groupwork successful is creating activities to which all students can contribute and from which all students can learn. These cases should focus on curriculum development for groupwork. Think of a specific lesson or unit you developed or adapted that included groupwork. Describe what you intended to teach. What were your goals? What student performances did you seek relative to your goals? What kinds of groupwork did you plan in order to achieve these goals? How, if at all, did you tailor the activities to the individual differences, backgrounds, and abilities of your students? What resources did you use to plan? Describe what happened when you taught the curriculum. How did students respond? Did they display the kind of thinking you sought? Were there any surprises? As you think back on this lesson, would you make any changes?

2. <u>Complexities of teaching</u>. Teaching concepts and skills using groupwork is generally regarded as more complicated than any traditional approach. Think of a lesson or unit during which you used groupwork that didn't work very well. What had you planned to teach? What group activities did you plan? Then describe your instruction in detail. Did you do anything special to encourage contributions from the lower achievers in your classroom? What happened during the groupwork? How did you handle the situation? As you think about the lesson, what would you do differently?

3. <u>Delegating authority</u>. One of the assumptions of effective groupwork is the importance of giving students responsibility for their own learning. Did you ever have a lesson or unit in which you felt uncomfortable giving so much power to your students? What were the circumstances? Tell your story. Describe in detail what students said and did. How did you handle the situation? Did you sense that your students might have felt uncomfortable or resistant to the new arrangement? Do you have any lingering questions about the redefinition of the traditional balance of power during these situations?

4. <u>Evaluation/accountability</u>. Evaluating the way students work in groups and the products of groupwork raises many dilemmas. Think of a time when you developed an approach to evaluating a groupwork activity. How did you decide which criteria to use? Did you assign grades or points to individuals and/or groups? What was your rationale? How did students respond to your criteria? How did you know whether students had learned the material? Do you continue to use this approach? If you have modified it, what changes have you made?

Interactions with Students

5. <u>Uncooperative students</u>. Do you have any individuals or groups of students who refuse to do work and are reluctant to participate in classroom activities (who either persistently act out or are withdrawn and apathetic toward school)? As a result, they aren't successful academically. You try several approaches of integrating them into group activities including, perhaps, designing special tasks in which they could contribute to their group—but the students continue to cause problems. (Or your new strategies pay off.) Tell your story.

6. <u>Low-status students</u>. Can you think of a student who never or rarely participates in groupwork and whose contributions are neither solicited nor valued? Describe the student's behavior in detail during a specific group activity. How did you account for his or her lack of participation? How did other students respond? What did you do? What effect did your action have on the student's contribution? How did the other students react to your intervention?

7. <u>Individualists</u>. Some students don't like to work in groups; they would much prefer to work on their own. Describe an event or series of events where a student or group of students refused to participate in the assigned group activity. How did you handle the situation? How did the student(s) respond? How did other students react? As you think about the situation, what might you do differently in the future?

Beyond the Classroom

8. <u>Parent–teacher conflict</u>. You are pleased with the way groupwork has influenced student learning in your classroom. On average, students are doing well on tests; they turn in creative assignments; they are developing critical thinking skills; and they appear to be enjoying their activities. But a parent or group of parents disapproves of group activities for their children. Tell your story.

9. <u>Administrative/collegial support</u>. Teachers who use groupwork often feel the need for support from colleagues and administrators. Think of a time when you felt overwhelmed by the logistics and demands of implementing groupwork. Did you have colleagues with whom to share your successes, doubts, and frustrations? Did you fail to get resources such as appropriate space and furniture, and hands-on materials? Did you fail to have time to prepare the activities and discuss your concerns with other teachers? How committed was your administrator to groupwork at your school? Tell your story. What impact did this support (or lack of) have on your teaching?

About the Editors

Judith H. Shulman is director of the Institute for Case Development at WestEd (formerly Far West Laboratory). Her research interests focus on the development of cases and their impact on teacher learning, the professional development of teachers, and the development of communities of learners. Her publications include *Case Methods in Teacher Education* (Teachers College Press), four coedited casebooks written by teachers, and numerous chapters and articles in professional journals. Ms. Shulman has conducted seminars on case methods throughout the United States and abroad and is an active member of several professional educational associations.

Rachel A. Lotan is co-director of the Program for Complex Instruction and senior research scholar at Stanford University School of Education. She received a Ph.D. in education and an M.A. in sociology from Stanford University. Prior to that she taught for 10 years and held various administrative positions in junior high and high schools in Israel. Her academic interests are sociology of the classroom, curriculum for heterogeneous classrooms, social organization of schools, and professional development of teachers. She is co-editor, with Elizabeth G. Cohen, of *Working for Equity in Heterogeneous Classrooms: Sociological Theory in Action* (Teachers College Press).

Jennifer A. Whitcomb is an assistant professor in the College of Education at the University of Denver and director of the Teacher Education Program. She completed her Ph.D. at Stanford University, where she studied the impact of case writing on teacher learning. Her research interests include teaching and teacher education, English education, groupwork instruction, and curriculum design and evaluation. Previously she taught English at middle school and high school levels.